CRITICAL PERSPECTIVES ON THE
ELECTORAL COLLEGE

ANALYZING THE ISSUES

CRITICAL PERSPECTIVES ON THE
ELECTORAL
COLLEGE

Edited by Bridey Heing

Enslow Publishing

101 W. 23rd Street
Suite 240
New York, NY 10011
USA

enslow.com

Published in 2020 by Enslow Publishing, LLC
101 W. 23rd Street, Suite 240, New York, NY 10011

Library of Congress Cataloging-in-Publication Data

Names: Heing, Bridey, editor.
Title: Critical perspectives on the electoral college / edited by Bridey Heing.
Description: New York: Enslow Publishing, 2020. | Series: Analyzing the
issues | Audience: For grades 7-12. | Includes bibliographical references
and index.
Identifiers: LCCN 2018024475| ISBN 9781978503311 (library bound) | ISBN
9781978505049 (paperback)
Subjects: LCSH: Electoral college—United States—Juvenile literature. |
Presidents—United States—Election—Juvenile literature.
Classification: LCC JK529 .H45 2019 | DDC 324.6/3—dc23
LC record available at https://lccn.loc.gov/2018024475

Printed in the United States of America

To Our Readers: We have done our best to make sure all website addresses
in this book were active and appropriate when we went to press. However,
the author and the publisher have no control over and assume no
liability for the material available on those websites or on any websites
they may link to. Any comments or suggestions can be sent by email to
customerservice@enslow.com.

Excerpts and articles have been reproduced with the permission of the
copyright holders.

Photo Credits: Cover Robert Daemmrich Photography Inc/Corbis
Historical/Getty Images; cover and interior pages graphics Thaiview/
Shutterstock.com (cover top, pp. 3, 6–7), gbreezy/Shutterstock.com
(magnifying glass), Ghornstern/Shutterstock.com (chapter openers).

CONTENTS

INTRODUCTION

In the United States, few political rituals are as important as presidential elections. Every four years voters across the country cast their ballots for a presidential ticket, setting the course for the nation. Or at least that's what many believe happens. Actually, voters are casting ballots that funnel to their state's Electoral College delegation, which in turn elects the president and vice president.

What is the Electoral College? Well, it's more of a process than an actual body. As outlined in the Constitution, the Electoral College is responsible for casting the deciding votes in the presidential election. To do so, states are responsible for setting rules on how electors are appointed, with their number being equal to the states' representation in Congress. Most states have a system by which the electors for their state are awarded to the candidate who wins the most votes in that state, known as a "winner-takes-all" system.

We often refer to the Electoral College to mean those electors, but it actually means the entire process surrounding the voting by those electors. While the national election takes place on the first Tuesday following the first Monday in November, state electors come together on the first Monday after the second Wednesday in December to cast their ballots. No federal law bars electors from casting their ballot as they choose rather than as their state says they must based on policy. Some states impose fines on electors who deviate, however, and it has been very rare for any elector to do so. The candidate with the majority of Electoral College votes is elected, and if no majority is reached the vote is held in the House of Representatives for president and the Senate for vice president.

Because of the Electoral College, our democracy is actually indirect, since our popular vote does not determine the winner of the election. This has been the root of controversy for years, as people argue that the Electoral College favors smaller states. In 2000 and 2016 the issue of the Electoral College became all the more important, as the winner of the popular vote during both elections did not win enough Electoral College votes to secure the presidency. Proponents of reform say this undermines our democracy and obscures the importance of voting.

But supporters of the Electoral College point to its place in the Constitution and the tradition that underpins it in our country. In this collection, we will read arguments from both sides of this complex debate, to understand the past, present, and possible futures of the Electoral College.

CHAPTER 1

WHAT THE EXPERTS SAY

The Electoral College may seem like a difficult thing to study. After all, it is only active for a brief period every four years. But there are many ways researchers and scholars can examine the Electoral College, from the way it functions to the impact it has on our government. Data scientists study the way votes within the Electoral College stack up against the popular vote, while constitutional scholars study the history of the institution and the legality of it moving forward. All of these angles are crucial for understanding the way we as citizens both influence and are influenced by the Electoral College, which we must know if we are to debate the future of this process in regard to future elections.

"HOW IS THE AMERICAN PRESIDENT ELECTED?," BY BRYAN CRANSTON, FROM THE *CONVERSATION*, OCTOBER 25, 2016

Just how democratic is the election for an American president?

You might think that the person who receives the most votes wins, right?

Wrong.

Just ask Al Gore, who in 2000 won more than half-a-million votes more than the "winner", George W. Bush.

In fact, on four occasions in American history (1824, 1876, 1888, and 2000), the winner of the presidential election actually received fewer votes than their opponent.

This is because, contrary to popular belief, voters do not actually elect the president.

Voters are merely indicating a preference for president, but the task of actually electing the president falls to 538 individual electors to the US Electoral College.

WHAT IS THE ELECTORAL COLLEGE?

To put it simply, each state is assigned a number of electors to the Electoral College, based on that state's delegation to the United States Congress.

There are 50 states.

Each state has two members of the US Senate, so there are 100 senators.

There are 435 members of the US House of Representatives, who are appointed by state on the basis of population, with each state having a minimum of one.

Therefore, the least populous states, such as Alaska and Wyoming, send three members to Congress - two senators and one representative. Conversely, the most populous state, California, sends two senators and 53 representatives, for a total of 55.

California's vote in the Electoral College is therefore 55.

This means that all 50 states send a total of 535 members to Congress.

In addition, the District of Columbia (Washington D.C.), sends one non-voting member to the House of Representatives (hence the slogan, "taxation without representation"), but no senators. However, when it comes to the Electoral College, D.C. is afforded the same number of votes as the smallest state - three.

The total votes in the Electoral College is therefore 538.

To win the presidency, a candidate needs an absolute majority vote in the Electoral College, which is half plus one, or 270. This is why you will hear a lot about the magic number "270" on Election Day.

If no one wins an absolute majority of the Electoral College, then the election is decided by a vote in the US House of Representatives, which has occurred on just one occasion (1824).

Electoral College "electors" are not usually members of Congress. Depending on the state, "electors" are elected by voters or state legislatures, or they are appointed.

ELECTION DAY VOTING

Forty-eight states, plus the District of Columbia, have a winner-takes-all approach to their Electoral College votes.

This means that on election day, if Hillary Clinton wins the popular vote in California by a single vote, she wins all of California's 55 Electoral College votes.

It therefore does not matter by how many votes Clinton or Trump win in each state, as long as they win more than the next person. A majority vote is not required, as the winner of the popular vote for each state by a plurality will win all of the electoral college votes.

There are two exceptions: Maine and Nebraska.

These two states award some of their electoral college votes on the basis of congressional district.

For example, Maine has two members of the House of Representatives, plus two senators, therefore it has four electoral college votes. One vote is awarded to whichever presidential candidate wins the most votes in each of the two congressional districts. The state's two "senatorial" votes are then awarded to whoever wins the most votes overall in the state. This is why in 2008, Barack Obama won a single vote from Nebraska, because he won one of Nebraska's three districts, while John McCain won the other two, and the state.

Confused? If you have made it this far, then you are almost an expert! Well done.

Long before election day, we know how most of the states will vote. For example, we know that Alabama will vote for Trump, and we know that Rhode Island will vote for Clinton. In fact, we already know what the result will be in approximately 40 states.

So candidates focus their campaigns on the remaining 10 states in which the outcome is less certain. These states comprise the so-called "swing" states, such as Florida, Ohio, Nevada, Virginia, and Colorado, plus a few others, like North Carolina, Missouri, and Indiana.

In the final two weeks before election day, it is these swing states that will receive all the attention from candidates.

So a presidential candidate is not aiming to win the popular vote across the country. They are not aiming to win all 50 states (although several have come close, such as Richard Nixon in 1972, and Ronald Reagan in 1984, each of whom won 49 states). A presidential candidate is aiming to win a majority of the Electoral College, in whatever shape that takes.

In 2012, Mitt Romney won 24 of 50 states (48%), and 47.2% of the national popular vote, but only won 38% of the electoral college vote.

When they devised the Constitution, the founding fathers did not believe that voters could be trusted to make the correct decision when voting. So the electoral college was conceived as a fail-safe. At the time, no voter in the electoral college was required to vote according to the result on election day. In 2016, there are 21 states that still do not require "electors" to adhere to the wishes of voters, but that is a whole other article.

1. According to the author, how does the Electoral College function in relation to elections?

2. How might it be possible for candidates with a larger popular vote total to lose the Electoral College?

"WHOSE VOTES COUNT THE LEAST IN THE ELECTORAL COLLEGE?" BY DALE R. DURRAN, FROM THE *CONVERSATION*, MARCH 13, 2017

In the days following the 2016 presidential election, many pundits and voters alike were stunned by the disparity between the popular vote, which went for Hillary Clinton, and the Electoral College, which favored Donald Trump.

If the president were elected by popular vote, every voter's ballot would have been given equal weight, or influence, over the outcome, and Hillary Clinton would have won. But, as evidenced by Donald Trump's victory, the Electoral College gives different weights to votes cast in different states. What are these weights, and how can we best compare them?

Most people believe the Electoral College weighs ballots in states with large populations much less than those in small states. For example, as the Washington Post noted shortly after the election, Wyoming has three electoral votes and a population of 586,107, while California has 55 electoral votes and 39,144,818 residents. Distributing the electoral vote evenly among each state's residents suggests that individual votes from Wyoming carry 3.6 times more influence, or weight, than those from California.

The electoral vote total for each state is determined by its population relative to other states, plus two more votes equal to its representation in the Senate. Yet focusing on state population is not the most useful way to determine the relative weight accorded each state's ballots. It does not help us understand how the weights assigned to voters by the Electoral College differ from the equal weights given to all voters in a popular vote. That's because the popular vote weighs each vote according to the total turnout, not the total population.

As a professor who studies how mathematics can be used to model weather using computers, I was curious to make an apples-to-apples comparison between the Electoral College and the popular vote. I did this by using the number of ballots cast, rather than population, to compare the weight given to voters in each state by the Electoral College.

Large states such as California, Texas and New York do comparatively well under this analysis; it is the midsized states that fare the worst. These unexpected results help us understand whose votes carry the least weight in U.S. presidential elections.

CRUNCHING THE NUMBERS

Roughly 136 million people voted in the 2016 presidential election. If we divide the total number of electoral votes – 538 – by the total number of voters, we can determine how much an individual vote counted toward an Electoral College vote. It turns out that, on a national average, each individual's vote counted for about four millionths of one full Electoral College vote.

To find the relative weight of a vote in each state, I divided each state's electoral vote total by the total number of ballots cast in that state, and then divided again by the exact fraction of an Electoral College vote accorded the average American voter (roughly four millionths). Let's call this the "vote weight," or simply the weight.

Note that, in a hypothetical system where the total electoral vote for each state equals the precise fraction of the total nationwide ballots cast in that state, votes in all states would be assigned weights of one, the same as in a national popular vote.

My calculations show voters in Wyoming did indeed receive the most weight, 2.97, for their votes. Voters in Florida came out on the bottom, with a voting weight of just 0.78. The weight given to the votes in Louisiana exactly matched the national average of one.

Two of the largest states, California and New York, came out only slightly below the national average. Votes from Texas, the second most populous state, actually received an above-average weight of 1.07.

Except for Florida, the states with the smallest weights are midsized, with between seven and 20 electoral votes each. For these states, there is no systematic relationship between vote weight and each state's electoral vote total.

The surprisingly low weights carried by votes in many midsized states are partly explained by the difference between the population – which determines the number of electoral votes – and the actual number of eligible voters in each state. Eligible voters do not include those who are too young to vote, noncitizens and, in some states, prisoners or former prisoners.

But it is voter turnout that primarily explains the low vote weights in states with seven or more electoral votes. In fact, the state-to-state difference in voter turnout was the most important factor in determining the variation of vote weights in midsized and large states in the 2016 presidential election.

In contrast to the weak relationship between a state's weight and its electoral vote total, the weight attached to each vote clearly tends to decrease as voter turnout within a state increases.

It is hardly surprising that higher turnout within a state decreases the weight accorded to each ballot, because the fixed number of electoral votes for any given state must be shared among the total number of ballots cast. But it does seem remarkable that the link between turnout and weight is so much stronger than the link between the number of electoral votes and weight.

For example, consider the difference between Oklahoma and Oregon. Both states have seven electoral votes, but their weights, 1.22 and 0.89, are quite different. That's primarily because only 52 percent of eligible voters turned out in Oklahoma – much less than the 66.6 percent turnout in Oregon. That gave Oklahomans a greater weight per vote in the Electoral College than their fellow citizens in Oregon.

In another example, South Carolina saw a relatively low 56.8 percent turnout, versus the much higher 69.8 percent turnout in Colorado. Both states have nine electoral votes. But, as a consequence of voter turnout, ballots in South Carolina received a weight of 1.09, while those in Colorado were given a much lower weight of 0.82.

As a final example, consider the pair of states with 29 electoral votes each: New York and Florida. New York's weight of 0.97 exceeds Florida's weight of 0.78, mostly because turnout in New York was 55.7 percent, while that in Florida was 64.5 percent.

UNTANGLING THE ELECTORAL COLLEGE

My analysis does not completely capture the many ways in which the Electoral College modifies the influence attached to individual votes.

For example, it does not take into account our winner-take-all system, where all of the electoral votes from each state are awarded to whoever wins the majority of the popular vote. (The congressional district method used in Maine and Nebraska has the same effect, just aggregated into smaller units.)

Consider the election's "battleground states," where the election was decided by about one percentage point or less. The relative weight of votes in four out of five of these states was less than 0.85.

The low weights for these states are largely due to high turnout, which was likely increased by the residents' awareness of the significance of their votes. While this increase in turnout did lower the weight of each vote in a battleground state, few would assert that the voters in these states had less opportunity to influence the presidential election than voters living in less competitive states with a high vote weight.

The way the Electoral College rewires American presidential elections in comparison to a simple popular vote is clearly complex. The Electoral College does add extra weight to votes cast in the least populated states. But the way this system treats voters in the remaining states is not well-understood. In states with seven or more electoral votes, it tends to weigh votes based on that state's voter turnout, rather than its number of electoral votes.

Whatever one's political affiliation, it is hard to be enthusiastic about a system that penalizes voters in high-turnout states.

1. How are electors in the Electoral College allocated?

2. What impact does that have on the power of individual votes?

EXCERPT FROM "ELECTORAL COLLEGE REFORM: CONTEMPORARY ISSUES FOR CONGRESS," BY THOMAS H. NEALE, FROM THE CONGRESSIONAL RESEARCH SERVICE, OCTOBER 6, 2017

SUMMARY

The electoral college method of electing the President and Vice President was established in Article II, Section 1 of the Constitution and revised by the Twelfth Amendment. It provides for election of the President and Vice President by electors, commonly referred to as the electoral college. A majority of 270 of the 538 electoral votes is necessary to win. For further information on the modern-day operation of the college system, see CRS Report RL32611, *The Electoral College: How It Works in Contemporary Presidential Elections*, by Thomas H. Neale.

The electoral college has been the subject of criticism and proposals for reform since before 1800. Constitutional and structural criticisms have centered on several of its features: (1) although today all electors are chosen by the voters in the presidential election, it is claimed to be not fully democratic, since it provides indirect election of the President; (2) it can lead to the election of candidates who win the electoral college but fewer popular votes than their opponents, or to contingent election in Congress if no candidate wins an electoral college majority; (3) it results in electoral vote under- and over-representation for some states between censuses; and (4) "faithless" electors can vote for candidates other than those they were elected to support. Legislative and political criticisms include (1) the general ticket system, currently used in all states except Maine and Nebraska, which is alleged to disenfranchise voters who prefer the losing candidates in the states; (2) various asserted "biases" that are alleged to favor different states and groups; and (3) the electoral college "lock," which has been claimed to provide an electoral college advantage to both major parties at different times.

In its defense, electoral college supporters claim that it is a fundamental component of federalism, that it has elected "the people's choice" in over 90% of presidential elections, and that it has promoted political stability and a broad-based, enduring, and generally moderate political party system.

Changing the electoral college system presents several options, sometimes characterized as: "end it," "mend it," or "leave it alone." Proposals to end the electoral college almost always recommend direct popular election, under which the candidates winning the most popular votes nationwide would be elected. In support of direct popular election, its advocates refer to the elections of 2000 and 2016, so-called electoral college "misfires," in which candidates were elected with an electoral college majority, but fewer popular votes than their principal opponents.

Almost all reform proposals—"mend it"—would keep electoral votes, but eliminate electors, thus ending the faithless elector phenomenon. They would then award the electoral votes directly by one of several methods: the general ticket system on a nationwide basis; the district system that awards electoral votes on a congressional district- and statewide-vote basis; or the proportional system that awards state electoral votes in proportion to the percentage of popular votes gained by each candidate. Despite more than 30 years of legislative activity from the 1940s through the late 1970s, proposed constitutional amendments did not win the approval of two-thirds of Members of both houses of Congress required by the Constitution for referral to the states.

Since 2004, some of the reforms identified above have been attempted in the states. District plan initiatives have been offered in California, Pennsylvania, Michigan, Virginia, and Wisconsin. Proportional plans have been proposed in Colorado and Pennsylvania. Nebraska has considered returning to the general ticket system. None of these, however, has been enacted to date.

A nongovernmental organization is currently promoting the National Popular Vote (NPV) initiative, an interstate compact that would effectively achieve direct popular election without a constitutional amendment.

It relies on the Constitution's broad grant of authority to the states in Article II, Section 1, to appoint presidential electors "in such Manner as the Legislature thereof may direct.... " States that join the compact pledge to award their electoral votes to the nationwide popular vote winners, regardless of who wins in their particular states. The compact would come into effect only after states controlling a majority of electoral votes (270 or more) were to join it. At the time of this writing, 10 states and the District of Columbia, which jointly control 165 electoral votes, have joined the NPV compact.

Since the 2016 presidential election, several amendments to eliminate the electoral college system and establish direct popular election have been introduced in the 114th and 115th Congress. For additional information on contemporary reform efforts, see CRS Report R44928, *The Electoral College: Reform Proposals in the 114th and 115th Congress*.

INTRODUCTION

The United States is unusual among contemporary presidential republics by providing for the indirect election of its President and Vice President.[1] Election of these two officers by a group of electors, known collectively as the electoral college, was established in Article II, Section 1 of the U.S. Constitution. The states were given blanket authority to appoint these electors "in such Manner as the Legislature[s] thereof" may direct. The original constitutional provisions, under which electors cast two votes for different candidates for President, but none for Vice President, proved unworkable[2] after only two contested elections,[3] resulting in a constitutional crisis during the deadlocked election of 1800.[4] Following this significant event, Congress proposed the Twelfth Amendment, which provides for separate electoral vote ballots in Congress for the President and Vice President, and which was ratified by the states in time for the 1804 election. The constitutional presidential election provisions of Article II, Section 1 and the Twelfth Amendment have remained unchanged since that time.

As with other provisions of the Constitution, Article II, Section 1 and the Twelfth Amendment established a basic framework for presidential elections but it extended considerable latitude to the states concerning its implementation. Arguably the most important related power reserved to the states was their right to appoint electors "in such Manner as the Legislature thereof may direct.... " In the years following ratification of the Twelfth Amendment, this right was exercised in various ways as state laws and political party procedures added a range of now-familiar additional elements to the system. These include such practices as

- popular election of electors by the voters;
- joint tickets for presidential and vice presidential candidates—the voter casts a single ballot for both candidates;
- the predominance of the general ticket, or winner-take-all, system or method, which awards all of a state's electoral votes to the ticket that wins the most popular votes statewide;
- a range of differing nomination procedures for elector candidates in the states; and,

- an enduring tradition that electors are expected, but not constitutionally required, to vote for the candidates to whom they are pledged.

The electoral college system has proved to be durable: 54 presidential elections have been held under this arrangement since the Twelfth Amendment was implemented in 1804. In 53 of these, it delivered a majority of electoral votes for President and Vice President,[5] and in 49 instances it delivered the presidency to "the people's choice," the candidates who won the most popular votes.[6] When measured by the first factor, it delivered an electoral vote majority to one candidate or ticket 98.2% of the times; when measured by whether it has delivered the presidency to "the people's choice," the candidate who won the most popular votes,[7] it did so 90.7% of the times. The electoral college has almost always been the subject of some criticism, however. Proposals to reform its alleged failings, or to replace it with something completely different, have been offered since the earliest days of the republic.

THE ELECTORAL COLLEGE IN BRIEF: A PRIMER

THE ELECTORAL COLLEGE IN PRINCIPLE: THE FOUNDERS' "ORIGINAL INTENT"

Few questions so vexed the Constitutional Convention of 1787 as that of presidential election. During the convention, the delegates voted successively for election by Congress;

direct popular election by the people; selection by the governors of the several states; election by electors chosen by the state legislatures; and even election by a group of Members of Congress chosen by lot.[8] At length, the matter was referred to a committee on "postponed matters," which reported a compromise plan near the close of the convention. The committee considered a range of generally agreed-upon principles for choice of the chief executive. Proceeding from the lengthy convention debate on choosing the chief executive, they contrived a mode of election designed to

- be free of undue influence by Congress, thus ensuring greater independence in the executive and separation of powers;
- provide a fundamental role for the states by establishing the election as a federal, as well as a national, process;
- allocate electors by a formula that provided a certain degree of advantage to less populous states, to avoid complete domination of the election process by the more populous ones;
- give the state legislatures broad authority over the choice of electors: at the legislatures' discretion, electors could be picked by popular vote, by the legislature itself, or by another body altogether; and, ultimately
- temper popular enthusiasms and partisan and sectional attachments by giving the actual vote to the electors, who, it was hoped, would be prominent citizens of their states and communities—well-informed and educated persons who would make a balanced and measured selection.

Notwithstanding the Founders' intentions, from the very beginning, the electoral college began to change, evolving through constitutional amendment, state laws, and political party practices. The growth of political parties and the spread of voting rights and democratic principles overtook the Founders' vision that the President would be chosen by the nation's most distinguished citizens. Within two decades, the electoral college evolved into the compound system that continues to govern U.S. presidential elections two centuries later.

THE ELECTORAL COLLEGE IN FORM: THE SYSTEM'S COMPONENTS AS THEY EXIST TODAY

As noted previously, the U.S. Constitution's minimal electoral college provisions have been complemented over the past two centuries by a range of federal and state laws, political party procedures, and enduring political traditions, resulting in the system as it exists today. The salient features of the contemporary arrangement, a mixture of these elements, are detailed below.

- The electors are collectively known as the electoral college; although this phrase does not appear in the Constitution, it gained currency in the early days of the republic, and was recognized in federal law in 1845.[9]
- The electoral college has no continuing existence. Its sole purpose is to elect the President and Vice President; electors convene in the state capitals, vote, and adjourn.
- Each state is allocated a number of electors equal to the combined total of its U.S. Senate and House of

Representatives delegations;[10] in addition, the District of Columbia is also allocated three electors.[11] At present, the total is 538, reflecting the combined membership of the Senate (100 Members), the House (435 Members), and the District of Columbia electors.

- Any person may serve as an elector, except Senators and Representatives, or any other person holding an office of "trust or profit" under the United States.[12]
- As noted previously, the state legislatures select the method by which electors are chosen.[13] In practice, all states currently provide for popular election of their electoral college delegations.[14] Candidates for the office of elector are nominated by political parties and other groups eligible to be on the ballot in each state. In most cases, the elector candidates are nominated by the state party committee or the party's state convention.[15]
- The winning presidential and vice presidential candidates must gain a majority of electoral votes (270 of 538) to be elected.
- If no ticket of candidates attains a majority, then the House of Representatives elects the President and the Senate elects the Vice President, in a procedure known as contingent election.

THE ELECTORAL COLLEGE IN FUNCTION: HOW IT WORKS IN CONTEMPORARY PRESIDENTIAL ELECTIONS

The assorted components of the electoral college system come into operation before, during, and after presidential election day, once every four years. Aside from the period of several months when electors are nominated, elected, and cast their votes, the college has no permanent or continuing existence.

- Presidential election day is set by federal law for Tuesday after the first Monday in November every fourth year succeeding the election of President and Vice President; one-third of U.S. Senators, all Members of the House of Representatives, and many state and local officials are also chosen on election day, which falls on November 3 in 2020.[17]
- On election day, voters across the country cast *one* vote for the team of presidential and vice presidential candidates they support. When they do so, they are actually voting for the political party "ticket" of candidates for the office of elector who support, and pledge to vote for, that party's presidential and vice presidential candidates.
- The popular vote is cast and certified, the electors are chosen, and they then assemble and vote in their respective states. While the nationwide popular vote count, the "horse race," is generally accorded widespread publicity during the campaign, ultimately it is the electoral vote tally in the states that decides the election.
- The goal of presidential campaigns is to win by carrying states that collectively cast a majority of electoral votes. In particular, political parties and presidential campaign organizations focus on states that are closely contested, that have large delegations of electoral votes, or both. Winning a majority of the more populous of these "battleground" or "swing"[18] states is considered crucial to obtaining the necessary electoral vote majority.

- In 48 states and the District of Columbia, the ticket that wins the most popular votes, a plurality or more, is awarded all the state's electoral votes. That is, the winning party's entire slate or ticket of candidates for the office of elector is elected. This is referred to as the "general ticket" or "winner-take-all" system or method.
- Maine and Nebraska use a different method, the "district" system, under which popular votes are counted twice; first, on a statewide basis, and second, on a congressional district basis. The presidential/vice presidential ticket receiving the most votes statewide receives two electors (or electoral votes) for this total. The ticket winning the most votes *in each congressional district* receives a single elector/electoral vote for that district. In this way, a state's electoral vote may be divided to reflect geographical differences in support within the state for different candidates.[19]
- Presidential electors assemble on the first Monday after the second Wednesday in December following the election.[20] In 2020, the electors are to assemble on December 14. They meet in their respective states and cast separate votes by paper ballot for the President and Vice President.[21]
- As noted earlier, candidates for the office of elector are selected by their respective political party. They are expected to vote for the candidates to whom they are pledged, but occasionally a "faithless elector" will vote against instructions.[22]
- After the electoral college votes, the results are forwarded by state officials to Congress and various other federal authorities designated by law. On January 6 of the year following a presidential election, Congress

meets in a joint session to count the electoral votes and make a formal declaration of which candidates have been elected President and Vice President.[23]

THE ELECTORAL COLLEGE IN SURVEY RESEARCH FINDINGS: TRENDS IN PUBLIC OPINION

Historically, public opinion, as measured by survey research, consistently supported reform (i.e., direct popular election), until recently.[24] The Gallup Poll reported as early as 1967 that 58% of respondents supported direct election, compared with 22% who favored retaining the electoral college; Gallup's 2013 survey recorded that 63% of respondents favored an amendment providing for direct election, while 29% favored retention of the electoral college.[25] Following the 2016 election, however, Gallup reported a shift to greater support for the electoral college system by respondents who identified themselves as "Republican" or "Lean Republican." Conversely, already high levels of support for direct popular election among respondents who identified themselves as "Democratic" or "Lean Democratic" rose to new heights in the post-2016 election Gallup Poll.[26]

ELECTORAL COLLEGE ISSUES

As noted in the introduction to this report, the electoral college and the system built around it have delivered a President and Vice President in 53 of 54 elections since the Twelfth Amendment was ratified in 1804. It has elected the candidates who received the most popular votes in 49 of those elections. While the system's defenders point to this as a considerable achievement, the electoral college has been criticized for a wide range of alleged failings since the earliest days of the republic. These criticisms fall generally in one of two categories. The first is essentially *philosophical*, and centers on the fact that the existing system is indirect, and provides a less than-fully democratic indirect election of the President and Vice President. The second category addresses perceived constitutional, legislative, and political structural flaws in the system asserted by its critics, focusing on the potential for various dubious procedures and outcomes, and the "biases" it is alleged to confer on certain groups and jurisdictions.

PHILOSOPHICAL CRITICISM: THE ELECTORAL COLLEGE PROVIDES INDIRECT ELECTION OF THE PRESIDENT

Perhaps the fundamental contemporary criticism of the Founders' creation is philosophical. Proponents of change maintain that the electoral college system is intrinsically undemocratic—it provides for "indirect" election of the President and Vice President. They assert that this is an 18th century anachronism, dating from a time when communications were poor, the literacy rate was much lower, and the nation had yet to develop the durable, sophisticated, and inclusive democratic political system it now enjoys. They maintain that only direct popular election of the President and Vice President is consistent with modern democratic values and practice.

Defenders of the electoral college system reject this suggestion; they maintain that while it may be indirect, it is not undemocratic—electors are chosen by the voters in free elections. They argue that the system prescribes a federal election of the President with votes tallied in each state, noting that the United States is a federal republic, not a plebiscitary democracy. The states, they assert, are long-established entities: distinct political, social, and economic communities that exercise substantial authority in many areas of governance, including presidential elections. The Founders, they note, intended that choosing the President would be an action Americans take both as citizens of the United States and as members of their state communities.[27]

STRUCTURAL CRITICISMS OF THE ELECTORAL COLLEGE SYSTEM

Beyond the fundamental claim that the electoral college is undemocratic, critics also cite what they identify as a wide range of structural flaws in the system; some of these are asserted to have origins in the constitutional provisions authorizing the electoral college system, while others are attributed variously to state legislation and political party practices.

CONSTITUTIONAL ISSUES

Some of the electoral college system's asserted failings are attributed by its critics to its structure and provisions as established in Article II, Section 1 of the Constitution and the Twelfth Amendment.

THE MINORITY PRESIDENT: AN ELECTORAL COLLEGE "MISFIRE"

Perhaps the most widely cited structural criticism of the electoral college system is that it can lead to the election of

Presidents and Vice Presidents who win a majority of the electoral vote, but who have gained fewer popular votes nationwide than their major opponents. This result has been variously referred to as "wrong winner" or an electoral college "misfire,"[28] particularly among reform advocates, and has occurred four times in the nation's history, 1876, 1888, 2000, and most recently in 2016.[29] In one other election, that of 1824, no candidate received a majority of electoral votes, leading to contingent election in Congress.[30] Proponents of direct election claim this potentially violates a fundamental democratic principle that the candidate winning the most popular votes should be elected. Electoral college supporters defend the system on the grounds that it is a federal election rather than a national plebiscite, and further note the system has delivered "the people's choice" in 49 of 54 elections since ratification of the Twelfth Amendment, a rate of 90.7%, as noted earlier in this report.

FAILURE TO GAIN AN ELECTORAL COLLEGE MAJORITY: CONTINGENT ELECTION

Contingent election, the electoral college "default" setting for cases in which no candidate receives the necessary majority of electoral votes, has also been cited by some as a structural failing of the system. If the presidential and/or vice presidential candidates fail to receive a simple majority of the electoral college votes, the Twelfth Amendment to the Constitution provides that the House of Representatives chooses the President and the Senate chooses the Vice President by contingent election.[31] In a contingent election, however, each state casts a single vote for President in the House, while each Senator casts a single vote for Vice President.[32]

Critics of contingent election generally argue that it removes the choice of President and Vice President one step further from the voters. That is, members of the House and Senate are free to exercise their choice without regard to the winners of the popular vote in their districts, states, or in the nation at large. Moreover, by effectively granting each state an equal vote, they claim that contingent election fails to account for great differences in population—and the number of popular votes cast—in the various states. Finally, it may be noted that the Twelfth Amendment does not provide for District of Columbia participation in a contingent election in the House and Senate. While the ratification of the Twenty-third Amendment in 1961 granted the District of Columbia three votes in the electoral college, the nation's capital would be effectively disenfranchised in a contingent election, as it is not a state and sends neither Senators nor Representatives to Congress. Defenders might counter by noting that contingent election is a "break glass only in case of an emergency" procedure, and has been required only once, under arguably unique circumstances,[33] in the 54 presidential elections since ratification of the Twelfth Amendment.

THE DECENNIAL CENSUS ISSUE

An additional structural issue is that the electoral college system bases allocation of electoral votes on the results of each decennial census. After each census, all 435 Members of the House of Representatives are reapportioned among the states: some states gain Representatives, others lose them, and some remain unchanged. Gains or losses in House seats lead to comparable adjustments to state electoral vote allocations following the census. For instance, the most notable adjustments following the 2010 census were Texas, which gained four House seats and whose electoral vote allocation rose from 34 to 38, and New York, which lost two House seats, and whose electoral vote allocation fell from 31 to 29. The decennial reallocation of electoral votes is reflected in the first presidential election following each census; for instance, electoral college reallocations resulting from the 2010 census were in place for the 2012 and 2016 elections, and will continue for the 2020 election.[34] Supporters of direct election note that decennial reapportionment of electors fails to account for significant population shifts that often occur *during* the course of a decade. Thus, the allocation of electoral votes for the elections of 2012, 2016, and 2020 reflect the 2010 population distribution among the states, but it makes no provision for changes during the decade. States that enjoy greater population gains during the current decade will not see those increases translated into more presidential electors until 2024. Until then, they will arguably be under-represented in the electoral college, while by the same logic, those that will ultimately lose seats and electors will be over-represented.

THE FAITHLESS ELECTOR

The Twelfth Amendment to the Constitution directs presidential electors to "meet in their respective States, and vote by ballot for President and Vice President, one of whom, at least, shall not be an inhabitant of the same state with themselves.... " It offers no further guidance beyond this instruction. There is ample evidence that the Founders intended electors to be representatives of their state political communities, free agents, able to vote for the persons they thought best fit for the presidency or vice presidency. Perhaps naively, they failed to anticipate the growth of partisanship and a nascent party system that emerged as early as President Washington's second Administration. The job of the elector was therefore quickly transformed from that of dispassionate judge to loyal party agent, expected to vote for the candidates designated by the party. So they remain today, and although nearly all electors since the earliest presidential elections have voted for the candidates to whom they were pledged, from time to time one or more electors have voted against the instructions of the electorate. Since the 1948 presidential election, 16 "faithless" or "unfaithful" electors have cast votes for candidates other than those to whom they were pledged, and one cast a blank ballot.[36]

Twenty-six states and the District of Columbia attempt to bind their electors by one of several means, generally by requiring an oath or pledge or requiring electors to vote for the candidates of the political party the elector represents.[37] In 1952, the Supreme Court held in *Ray v. Blair* that political parties could exercise state-delegated authority to require elector-candidates for the office of elector to pledge to support the party's presidential and vice presidential nominees.[38] The Court did not, however, rule on the constitutionality of state laws that bind electors. Many commentators suggest that binding electors and the pledges that electors make are constitutionally unenforceable, and that electors remain free agents who may vote for any candidate they choose.[39] In the presidential election of 2016, however, three would-be faithless electors were prevented from voting for candidates other than those to whom they were pledged.[40]

From the standpoint of electoral college defenders, it may be noted that 9,675 electoral votes have been cast in the 18 presidential elections held since 1948. Of these, the 16 that were indisputably cast against voters' instructions comprised less than two thousandths of one percent (0.001654%) of the total and had no effect on the outcome of any election.[41]

LEGISLATIVE AND POLITICAL ISSUES

The second category of asserted distortions caused by the electoral college arrangement stems from procedures that have been added to its constitutional provisions by the states over a long period of time. The most important issue is the nearly universal adoption of the general ticket, or winner-take-all, system for awarding electoral votes.

THE GENERAL TICKET SYSTEM—"WINNER TAKE ALL"

The general ticket system of awarding electoral votes is cited by critics as a structural failing of the electoral college system, an issue that does not stem from the Constitution, but rather from state laws. At the present time, 48 states and the District of Columbia provide that the ticket of presidential and vice presidential candidates that wins the most popular votes wins all the electoral votes for that jurisdiction. By awarding all of a state's electoral votes to the winner, regardless of the closeness of the popular vote results, the general ticket system is said to discount the votes of citizens who preferred the candidates receiving fewer votes. This asserted inequity is said to be particularly apparent in states where the popular vote is closely divided.[42] Conversely, electoral college defenders claim the general ticket system's "multiplier" effect tends to reinforce the overall election results by magnifying the winning ticket's margin and to deter frivolous challenges to the state-by-state results.[43]

Maine and Nebraska provide the only exceptions to the general ticket system, having established what is referred to as the "district system" of awarding electoral votes. In these states, as noted earlier in this report, votes are counted both by congressional district and on the statewide level. The candidates winning the most popular votes statewide are awarded the two electoral votes reflecting the state's "senatorial" electors, while the candidates winning in each congressional district are awarded one elector, reflecting the results in that district.[44] Proponents of direct election criticize the district system on the grounds that adding the "senatorial" electors to the statewide winners' total has much the same effect of disadvantaging the losing candidates and their supporters. District system supporters claim that it better reflects geographical differences in candidate support throughout a state, thus delivering an electoral vote that more accurately represents local preferences.

ALLEGED BIASES OF THE ELECTORAL COLLEGE SYSTEM

Opponents of the electoral college identify another category of alleged distortion built into the system. These are said to provide an advantage derived from state population or voter characteristics or behavior.

As the composition of the electoral college is partially based on state representation in Congress, some maintain it is inconsistent with the "one person, one vote" principle.[45] The Constitutional Convention agreed on a compromise plan whereby less populous states were assured of a minimum of three electoral votes, based on two Senators and one Representative, regardless of state population. Since electoral college delegations are equal to the combined total of each state's Senate and House delegation, its composition is arguably weighted in favor of the "small," or less populous, states. The two "senatorial" or "at large" electors to which each state is entitled are said to confer on them an advantage over more populous states, because voters in the less populous ones cast more electoral votes per voter. For instance, in 2016, voters in Wyoming, the least populous state, cast 255,849 popular votes and three electoral votes for President, or one electoral vote for every 85,283 voters. By comparison, Californians cast 14,181,595 popular votes and 55 electoral votes, or one electoral vote for every 257,847 voters.[46] As a result of this distribution of electoral votes among the states, it is argued that "small" states have an advantage over large states because their electoral vote totals are larger in proportion to their population.[47]

While it is generally recognized, as noted above, that small states possess an *arithmetical* advantage in the electoral college, some observers hold that, conversely, the most populous (large) states enjoy a *voting power* advantage, because they control the largest blocs of electoral votes. In combination with the general ticket system, this is said to confer an advantage on voters in these states because the large blocks of electoral votes they control have greater ability to influence the outcome of presidential elections. To use the previously cited example, a voter in Wyoming in 2016 could influence only three electoral votes, 1.1% of the 270 electoral votes needed to win the presidency, whereas a voter in California could influence 55 electoral votes in the same presidential election, 20.4% of the votes needed to gain an electoral college majority. According to this argument, known as the "voting power" theory, the electoral college system actually provides an *advantage* to the most populous states, and disadvantages all other states and the District of Columbia.[48]

Another theory centers on an asserted advantage enjoyed by ethnic minority voters. According to this argument, minority voters, principally African Americans, Latinos, and Jews, tend to be concentrated in populous states with large electoral college delegations. By virtue of this concentration, they are said to exert greater influence over the outcomes in such states because their voting patterns tend to favor candidates whose policies they perceive to be in their interest, thus helping win the states and their electoral votes for these candidates.[49]

A further alleged bias in the electoral college system is said to stem from the constitutional mandate that

Representatives shall be apportioned among the several States according to their respective numbers, *counting the whole number of persons in each state* (emphasis added), excluding Indians not taxed.

Except for the two "senatorial electors,"[51] a state's electoral vote allocation depends on the number of Representatives in Congress apportioned to it. A state's electoral vote is based to this extent on *residents*, not on *citizens*, and therefore, it is asserted that states that have high numbers of noncitizen residents counted in the Census enjoy a bias in the allocation of both Representatives and electoral votes.[52] For instance, the United States Election Project estimated that in 2016, 16.7% of California's population was noncitizens, the highest proportion of any state, followed by Texas at 13.5% and Nevada at 12.6%.[53] Critics of the current method have argued that counting noncitizens for the purposes of apportionment of Representatives and presidential electors provides an unfair advantage to states with large non-citizen populations.[54] A 2012 *Washington Post* article discussing this alleged bias concluded that, due to large concentrations of noncitizens, California gained five electors from the 2010 reapportionment that it would not have received if Representatives and electoral votes were allocated according to *citizen* population, rather than *resident* population. According to this calculation, Texas gained two additional electors and New York, Florida, and Washington each gained one because Representatives are apportioned according to population. Conversely, the author calculated that Indiana, Iowa, Louisiana, Michigan, Missouri, Montana, Ohio, Oklahoma, and Pennsylvania each lost one elector due to the noncitizen population advantage.[55]

Another alleged advantage or bias of the electoral college centers on differing rates of voter participation in the states. Neal Peirce and Lawrence Longley, writing in

The People's President, suggested that voters in states that have lower rates of participation may enjoy an advantage because it takes fewer popular votes per elector to win the state and all its electoral votes.[56] For instance, in the 2016 election, Hawaii, with four electoral votes, had the lowest rate of voter participation: 42.2% of eligible voters participated, casting 428,937 votes for President, a figure that equals 107,234 votes for each elector. By comparison, Minnesota, with 10 electoral votes, had the highest rate of participation, 74.2% of eligible voters, who cast 2,944,813 votes for President, a figure that equals 294,481 votes per elector.[57]

These various biases have been debated over the years. For instance, the alleged minority vote advantage was advanced by the Presidents of the American Jewish Congress and the National Urban League[58] as a reason for their support of the electoral college system during hearings before the Senate Judiciary Committee's Subcommittee on the Constitution during its 1979 consideration of direct election amendment,[59] while Alexander Bickel also supported the electoral college in this context.[60] Conversely, other commentators have sought to refute many of the "biases" of the electoral college system.[61]

THE "ELECTORAL COLLEGE LOCK"

A final asserted bias considered in this report is the so-called "electoral college lock," a perceived phenomenon identified in the late 1960s that was claimed to provide a long-term election advantage to the candidates of a particular party, originally to Republicans, and later, Democrats, at least through the 2016 election. The lock was loosely defined as a tendency of the system to favor presidential candidates of one party over another. It was said to operate because a bloc of states possessing a large, sometimes decisive, number of electoral votes could be reliably expected to vote in successive elections for the candidates of the political party that tended to dominate those states. For instance, California is regarded as a reliably Democratic or "blue" state in presidential elections, one that dependably delivers its 55 electoral votes to the Democratic Party presidential candidates. Texas is similarly cited as a "red" state that reliably produces its 36 electoral votes for Republican presidential candidates.[62] These one-word descriptors quickly gained currency during the first decade of the 21st century, and have since become a standard verbal identifier for defining a state's political record and voting patterns.

As with other electoral college issues, the electoral college lock was also said to be dependent on the general ticket system discussed earlier in this report, because it delivers a state's entire electoral vote to the winning candidates.

The electoral college lock theory dates to the late 1960s, when analyst and historian Kevin Philips developed a thesis that political and social developments were responsible for a partisan realignment that was arguably the most important factor in creating the lock. In *The Emerging Republican Majority*, he predicted that growing Republican Party conservatism and the Democratic Party's embrace of the civil rights movement and a socially and politically progressive or liberal agenda would combine with demographic developments favorable to the "Sunbelt" states to produce a restructuring of the nation's political balance in favor of the Republican Party.[63] Political commentators generally credit Horace Busby, a political advisor to

President Lyndon B. Johnson, with naming rights for the lock.[64] During the 1980 presidential election campaign, Busby reviewed electoral college trends since the 1968 election and concluded that "... Democratic candidacies for the White House may no longer be viable. *The Republican lock (emphasis* added) is about to close; it will be hard for anyone to open ... between now and the year 2000."[65]

At the time Busby coined the term electoral college lock, the phenomenon was largely presumed to benefit the Republican Party. For a period of at least 20 years, beginning in 1968, observers pointed to a nearly uninterrupted string of GOP presidential election victories as proof of the lock.[66] Republican candidates won five of six elections during this period, taking an average of 417 of 538 electoral votes per election.[67]

In the years following the 2008 and 2012 presidential elections, some observers discerned a shift in the electoral college lock in favor of Democratic Party presidential candidates.[68] They noted that Democratic candidates had won four of the previous six presidential elections (1992, 1996, 2008 and 2012) by convincing electoral college margins, taking an average of 327 electoral votes per election.[69] In addition, it was noted that 18 states disposing of 242 electoral votes, sometimes referred to as "the blue wall,"[70] had voted Democratic in all six.[71] This tendency was said to provide both a structural electoral vote advantage for Democratic candidates, and a serious obstacle to Republicans in these contests.[72] It was attributed in part to the fact that social attitudes in the general public were said to have grown more favorable to Democratic candidates, and that, as one observer claimed, "the demographic pendulum is swinging toward the Democrats. Young voters,

Hispanics and a more active African-American electorate added states like Nevada, New Mexico, Colorado and Virginia to President Obama's winning coalition in the past two elections."[73]

Other observers, however, cautioned against accepting the electoral college lock as an inevitable process that would advantage its current beneficiary notwithstanding other influences. They claimed that the purported Republican lock of the 1960s through 1980s, and the perceived Democratic lock that began in the 1990s were not a deterministic phenomenon, but could also be attributed to, and influenced by, a wide range of factors, including such influences as domestic social and economic conditions, international issues affecting public attitudes toward national security, U.S. involvement in conflict abroad, scandals of various sorts, candidate popularity, "time for a change"[74] sentiment, and even the competence, or lack thereof, of a presidential nominee's campaign.[75]

The 2016 presidential election arguably confirmed some of these cautions about the inevitability of the electoral college lock or the durability the "blue wall," given that three of the claimed blue wall states, Michigan, Pennsylvania, and Wisconsin, voted for the Republican candidates, providing a combined total of 46 electoral votes to the GOP ticket, thus ensuring its election.[76]

ELECTORAL COLLEGE REFORM OPTIONS: END IT? MEND IT? LEAVE IT ALONE?

Congress may consider three basic options if it addresses the question of electoral college reform. The first choice, widely advocated for at least 50 years, would repeal the sections of the Constitution dealing with the electoral college—clause 2 of Article II, Section 1 and the Twelfth Amendment—and substitute direct popular election. The second, largely dormant for several decades, would reform the electoral college system by eliminating some of the alleged problem areas cited in the previous section of this report. A third option would be to leave arrangements as they are at present.

END IT—DIRECT POPULAR ELECTION REPLACES THE ELECTORAL COLLEGE

The direct election alternative would abolish the electoral college, substituting a single nationwide count of popular votes. The candidates winning a plurality, or a majority, of the votes cast would be elected President and Vice President. Most direct election proposals would constitutionally mandate today's familiar joint tickets of presidential/vice presidential candidates, a feature that is already incorporated in state law.[77] Some would require simply that the candidates that gain the most popular votes be elected, while others would set a minimum threshold of votes necessary to win election—generally 40% of votes cast. Some proposals would require a majority to elect, and if no presidential ticket were to win either a majority or 40% of the popular vote, then the two tickets with the highest popular vote total would compete in a subsequent runoff election. Alternatively, some versions of the direct popular election plan would provide for Congress, meeting in joint session, to elect the President and Vice President if no ticket reached the 40% or majority threshold.

DIRECT ELECTION—DISCUSSION

Proponents of direct popular election cite a number of factors in support of the concept, many of which address the issues cited in the previous sections of this report. As their core argument, they assert that the process would be simple, national, and democratic. They maintain that direct popular election would provide for a single, democratic choice, allowing all the nation's voters to choose the President and Vice President directly, with no intermediaries. The "people's choice" would always be elected. According to supporters of direct election, every vote would carry the same weight in the election, no matter where in the nation it was cast. No state or group of voters would be advantaged, nor would any be disadvantaged. Direct election would eliminate the potential complications that could arise under the current system in the event of a presidential candidate's death between election day and the date on which electoral vote results are declared, since the winning candidates would become President-elect and Vice President-elect as soon as the popular returns were certified.[78] All other procedures of the existing system, such as provisions in law for certifying the electoral vote in the states and the contingent election process, would be replaced by these comparatively simple requirements.

Critics of direct election and electoral college defenders seek to refute these arguments. Direct election proponents claim their plan is more democratic and provides for "majority rule," yet most direct election proposals require only a plurality—as little as 40% of the vote—in order to elect the President. Other versions include no minimum vote threshold at all, or provide for election by Congress in these circumstances. How, they might ask, could plurality Presidents or those elected by Congress, a practice that was rejected by the Founders, be reconciled with the ideal of strict majoritarianism?[79] Opponents might further maintain that direct election would result in political fragmentation, as various elements of the political spectrum form competing parties, and regionalism, as numerous splinter candidates claiming to champion the particular interests of various parts of the country, entered presidential election contests. Further, they assert that direct election would foster acrimonious and protracted post-election struggles, rather than eliminate them. A runoff election would, they might suggest, simply offer more incentives to bargaining and intrigue, thus confirming the founders' worst fears. Under direct election, they suggest, every close election might resemble the bitter post-election contests in 2000, not just in one state, but nationwide, as both parties seek to gain every possible vote. They contend that such rancorous disputes could have profound negative effects on political comity in the nation, and might ultimately undermine public confidence in the legitimacy of the presidency and federal government.[80]

MEND IT—REFORM THE ELECTORAL COLLEGE

Reform measures that would retain the electoral college in some form have included several variants. Most versions of these plans share certain common elements. They would

- eliminate the office of presidential elector while retaining electoral votes;
- award electoral votes directly to the candidates, without the action of electors; and
- retain the requirement that a majority of electoral votes is necessary to win the presidency.

In common with direct election, most would also require joint tickets of presidential-vice presidential candidates, a practice currently provided by state law. The three most popular reform proposals include

- the automatic plan or system, which would mandate the assignment of electoral votes automatically on the current general ticket/winner-take-all basis in each state and the District of Columbia;
- the district plan or system, as currently adopted in Maine and Nebraska, which would automatically award one electoral vote to the winning ticket in each congressional district in each state, but would also automatically assign each state's two additional "senatorial" electoral votes to the statewide popular vote winners; and
- the proportional plan or system, which would automatically award each state's electoral votes in proportion to the percentage of the popular vote gained by each ticket.[81]

ELECTORAL COLLEGE REFORM—DISCUSSION

Supporters of the electoral college, as presently structured, or reformed, offer various arguments in its defense.[82]

They reject the suggestion that it is undemocratic: electors are chosen by the voters in free elections, and have been in nearly all instances since the first half of the 19th century. They cite the electoral college as a major component of federalism, noting that the Constitution prescribes a federal election of the President by which votes are tallied in each state. As a federal republic, they assert the states have a legitimate role in many areas of governance, and that the founders intended that in choosing the President voters act both as citizens of the United States, and as members of their state communities. Proponents of the electoral college maintain that the assignment of two electors to each state regardless of population is an additional "federal" component of the presidential election system, comparable to the two Senators assigned by the Constitution to each state. Further, they maintain the electoral college system promotes political stability. Parties and candidates must conduct ideologically broad-based campaigns throughout the nation in order to assemble a majority of electoral votes. The consequent need to forge national coalitions having a wide appeal has been a contributing factor in the moderation and stability of the two-party system. They find the "faithless elector" argument to be specious: as noted previously in this report, few votes have been cast against instructions, and none has ever influenced the outcome of an election. Moreover, nearly all electoral college reform plans would remove even this slim possibility for mischief by eliminating the office of elector. On a practical level, they note that the general ticket system generally magnifies the winning ticket's electoral vote margin, an action they claim tends to bring closure to the election process and promote the legitimacy of the winning candidates.[83]

Supporters of direct election and critics of the electoral college counter that the existing system is cumbersome, potentially anti-democratic, and beyond saving. As noted earlier they maintain that the existing arrangement is the antithesis of their simple and democratic proposal. Its worst flaw has thwarted the public will on four occasions, by electing as President a candidate who received fewer popular votes than his principal opponent, and by throwing election into the House of Representatives in a fifth. They find the Twelfth Amendment's contingent election provisions to be even less democratic than the primary provisions of Article II, Section 1 of the Constitution.[84] They cite the decennial Census issue, the provision of "senatorial" electors regardless of state population, the prospect of the faithless elector, and the general ticket system as providing opportunities for political mischief and deliberate distortion of the voters' choice. They warn that although all states currently provide for choice of electors by popular vote, state legislatures still retain the constitutional option of taking this decision out of the voters' hands, and selecting electors by some other, less democratic means.[85] This option was discussed in Florida in 2000 during the post-election recounts,[86] and its survival they claim confirms their argument that even one of the more "democratic" features of the electoral college system is not guaranteed, and could be changed arbitrarily by politically motivated state legislators.

LEAVE IT ALONE

For nearly 30 years, the issue of electoral college reform held a prominent place on the agenda of successive Congresses. Between the late 1940s through 1979, hundreds of electoral college reform proposals were introduced in both chambers. They embraced a wide range of approaches to the question, but generally followed the outlines set out in the previous section: "ending it" by eliminating the entire electoral college system and establishing direct popular election, or "mending it" by reforming its more controversial provisions. The question of electoral college reform or replacement was actively considered throughout these years. Proposed amendments were the subject of hearings in the Senate and House Judiciary Committees on 17 different occasions between 1948 and 1979, and, most notably, electoral college reform proposals were debated in the full Senate on five occasions, and twice in the House during this period. Proposals were approved by the necessary two-thirds majority twice in the Senate and once in the House, but never the same amendment in the same Congress.[87]

Following the 1979 defeat of a direct popular election amendment on the Senate floor, and the subsequent departure of prominent congressional advocates, the question of electoral college reform largely disappeared from public attention and Congress's legislative agenda. The Senate's failed vote on a direct popular amendment marked the last occasion on which either chamber took floor action on an electoral college reform measure of any kind. Reform or replacement proposals had been familiar items on the congressional agenda; for instance, 26 amendments were introduced to abolish or reform the electoral college in the 96th Congress (1979-1980). In the ensuing years, however, the number of related constitutional amendments introduced in the House or Senate dropped from an average of eight per Congress for the 101st through 110th Congresses, to none in the 113th Congress (2013-2014).

In 2016, however, as noted previously, according to official state returns reported by the Federal Election Commission, a President and Vice President were elected with a majority of electoral votes, but fewer popular votes than their principal opponents. The recurrence of this outcome in 2016 contributed to renewed interest among some in replacing the electoral college with direct popular election. Following the election, four proposals to establish direct popular election were introduced in the last weeks of the 114th Congress, To date in the 115th Congress, two amendments to establish direct popular election have been introduced: H.J.Res. 19, offered on January 5, 2017, by Representative Steve Cohen, would replace the electoral college with direct popular election of the President and Vice President by plurality vote. It would also authorize Congress to set voter qualifications, times, places, and manner of holding presidential elections, and other election-related policies. H.J.Res. 65, the "Every Vote Counts Amendment," introduced by Representative Gene Green on February 7, 2017, provides for direct popular election by plurality, and also provides Congress with additional authority over related activities. Both resolutions have been referred to the House Committee on the Judiciary and to its Subcommittee on the Constitution and Civil Justice. For additional information and analysis of current electoral college reform or replacement proposals, see CRS Report R44928, *The Electoral College: Reform Proposals in the 114th and 115th Congress*, by Thomas H. Neale.

TRENDS IN CONGRESSIONAL ELECTORAL COLLEGE REFORM PROPOSALS

Two trends are identifiable within the context of congressional proposals to reform or replace the electoral college introduced since the late 20th century. First, proposed amendments introduced in the past decade all embraced the "end it" option, substituting direct popular election for the electoral college; no proposal to reform the electoral college has been introduced since the 107th Congress (2001-2003). Second, the scope of proposed direct popular election amendments has arguably grown in complexity and detail.

Given the contemporary context, it may be that the first development reflected a decline in electoral college support, lack of interest in reform proposals, or simply the absence of a sense of urgency. It is arguable that supporters of the current system would coalesce to defend the electoral college if its existence or integrity were endangered. Actions by the Heritage Foundation and the State Government Leadership Foundation identified later in this report arguably confirm this thesis.

The second trend is that recent proposed amendments not only provided for direct popular election, but also included provisions to enhance and extend federal authority in such areas as residence standards, definition of citizenship, national voter registration, inclusion of U.S. territories and other associated jurisdictions in the presidential election process, establishment of an election day holiday, and ballot access standards for parties and candidates. If approved and ratified, provisions such as these would provide Congress with enhanced authority to establish broad national election standards, potentially superseding current state and political party practices and requirements, at least with respect to federal elections.[88]

The prospect of increased federal involvement in the administration of presidential elections raises two potential issues. The first is whether such federal involvement in traditionally state and local practices would impose additional responsibilities and uncompensated costs on state and local governments. If so, such requirements might be considered to be unfunded mandates, as they could impose additional costs on sub-federal governments, and as such would be subject to points of order on the floor of both the House and Senate.[89] One response by the affected state and local governments might be to call for federal funding to meet the increased expenses imposed by federal requirements. Precedent for this exists in the grant program incorporated in the Help America Vote Act of 2002 (HAVA).[90] An additional issue centers on perceptions that such an amendment and resultant legislation might be regarded as federal intrusion in state and local responsibilities. For instance, a far-reaching scenario could include the gradual assumption of the election administration structure by the federal government. In this hypothetical case, questions could be raised as to (1) the costs involved; (2) whether a national election administration system could efficiently manage all the varying nuances of state and local conditions; and (3) what would be the long-term implications for federalism. Conversely, it could be asserted that (1) a national or federal election administration structure is appropriate for national elections; (2) state or local concerns are counterbalanced by the urgent requirement that every citizen be enabled and encouraged to vote; and (3) every vote should be accurately counted.

ACTION AT THE STATE LEVEL SINCE 2008

While Congress has not taken significant action on the question of electoral college reform in recent years, there has been considerable activity in the states.

Only an amendment can alter the constitutional structure of the electoral college, but the states retain considerable authority concerning various aspects of the system. For instance, as noted elsewhere in this report, Article II, Section 1, clause 2 gives the state legislature broad authority to "appoint" electors in any way they choose.

In practice, this appointment has been by popular election for 150 years. States also have authority over the formula by which electors are elected; as noted, 48 states and the District of Columbia use the general ticket system, but Maine and Nebraska adopted the district system or plan decades ago, an example of the states acting in their classic role as "laboratories of democracy."

In other words, the states are free to experiment with systems of elector selection and electoral vote allocation, up to a point. Over the past decade, both proportional and congressional district plan proposals have been advanced in the states, as identified in the following section, but none has been successfully adopted to date. These have included efforts in the following states:

- **California**—Ballot initiative campaigns in 2008 (the California Presidential Reform Act) and 2012 (the California Electoral College Reform Act) sought to establish a district system of electoral vote distribution and in 2014 (the California Split Electoral College Vote Distribution Initiative) to establish a proportional system by popular vote, but all three failed to gain ballot access.[91]

- **Colorado**—On November 2, 2004, Colorado voters rejected a state constitutional amendment, Amendment 36, which would have provided a proportional allocation of electoral votes.[92] After a contentious campaign that gained a degree of national interest, the proposal was ultimately defeated by the voters.[93]

- **Michigan**—In 2011 and 2014, bills were introduced in the legislature to change electoral vote allocation in Michigan from the general ticket to the district system. No action beyond hearings was taken on either proposal.[94]

- **Nebraska**—Bills to return Nebraska from the district system to the general ticket allocation of electoral votes were introduced in the state's unicameral legislature several times after 2011, most recently in 2016. None of these proposals has been successful to date.[95]

- **Pennsylvania**—In 2011 and 2012, two proposals were introduced in the Pennsylvania legislature to award the commonwealth's electoral votes according to the district system, but neither bill was enacted.[96] In 2013, legislation was introduced to award electoral votes according to the proportional system. As with earlier proposals, no action was taken beyond committee referral.[97]

- **Virginia**—In 2012, a variant of the district system was introduced in the Virginia General Assembly. In contrast to the system as enacted in Maine and Nebraska, which awards each state's two senatorial electors to the presidential ticket *winning the most popular votes statewide*, this legislation would have awarded the senatorial electors to the presidential ticket that won the popular vote *in the greatest number of congressional districts statewide*.[98] The bill was "bypassed indefinitely" in 2013.[99]
- **Wisconsin**—Between 2011 and 2014, press accounts indicated that Wisconsin state legislators would introduce legislation to award the state's electoral votes according to the district system. The Wisconsin Legislature's database for this period does not, however, identify any such proposal as having been introduced.[100]

In addition to these specific plans, other states have been reported as considering changes to their current allocation of electoral votes in recent years, particularly Ohio and Florida. At the time of this writing, however, no measure has been introduced in the legislature of either state to this effect, and press accounts indicate that such actions are unlikely in the immediate future.[101]

Related activity in state legislatures continued following the 2016 presidential election. According to press reports, bills to change from the general ticket to district systems were introduced in 2017 in the legislatures of Minnesota and Virginia.[102] At the time of this writing, neither proposal has progressed beyond committee assignment in the respective legislatures.[103]

NGO PROPOSAL: THE NATIONAL POPULAR VOTE INITIATIVE

Another contemporary electoral college reform or replacement effort centers on the National Popular Vote initiative, (NPV), a non-governmental campaign. NPV is a nongovernmental initiative which seeks to establish direct popular election of the President and Vice President through an interstate compact, rather than by constitutional amendment.[104] Under the compact's provisions, legislatures of signatory states (including the District of Columbia) would appoint presidential electors committed to the presidential *ticket that gained the most votes nationwide.* Assuming all 50 states joined the NPV compact, this would deliver a unanimous electoral college decision for the candidates winning the most popular votes.

Northwestern University law professor Robert W. Bennett and constitutional law professors Akhil and Vikram Amar are generally credited as originators of the NPV concept.[105] NPV relies on the Constitution's broad grant (in Article II, Section 1, clause 1) of power to each state to "appoint, *in such Manner as the Legislature thereof may direct* [emphasis added], a Number of Electors, equal to the whole Number of Senators and Representatives to which the State may be entitled in the Congress."[106]

Specifically, the plan calls for an interstate compact in which the legislatures in each of the participating states agree to appoint electors pledged to the candidates who won the *nationwide popular vote*. State election authorities would count and certify the popular vote in each state, which would be aggregated and certified nationwide as the "nationwide popular vote." The participating state legislatures would then choose the slate of electors pledged to the "nationwide popular vote winner," *notwithstanding the results within their particular state*.[107] Barring unforeseen circumstances, if all 50 states and the District of Columbia were to join the NPV, it would yield a unanimous electoral college vote of 538 electors for the winning candidates.

The compact, however, would take effect only if states controlling a majority of the electoral college, 270 or more votes, were to approve the plan. This would guarantee the plan's success by ensuring that at least 270 electoral votes would be cast for the candidates winning the most popular votes.

If the national popular vote were tied, the states would be released from their commitment under the compact, and would choose electors who represented the presidential ticket that gained the most votes in each particular state.

One novel NPV provision would enable the presidential candidate who won the national popular vote to fill any vacancies in the electoral college with electors of his or her own choice.

States would retain the right to withdraw from the compact, but if a state chose to withdraw within six months of the end of a presidential term, the withdrawal would not be effective until after the succeeding President and Vice President had been elected.

Between 2007 and 2014, 10 states and the District of Columbia joined the compact. They are allocated a total of 165 electoral votes, 61% of the 270 vote majority that would be required for the compact to be implemented. States that have adopted the NPV Compact, including their electoral vote allotments, are listed below, in chronological order.

- Hawaii (4 electoral votes), 2008;
- Illinois (20 electoral votes), 2008;
- Maryland (10 electoral votes), 2008;
- New Jersey (14 electoral votes), 2008;
- Washington (12 electoral votes), 2009;
- Massachusetts (11 electoral votes), 2010;
- District of Columbia (3 electoral votes), 2010;
- Vermont (3 electoral votes), 2011;
- California (55 electoral votes), 2011;
- Rhode Island (four electoral votes), 2013; and
- New York (29 electoral votes), 2014.

According to National Popular Vote, Inc., the national advocacy group for the NPV initiative, the compact has been introduced in all 50 states and the District of Columbia.[108] The National Conference of State Legislatures reports that in 2017 it is "pending" in the legislatures of eight states that jointly dispose of 88 electoral votes.[109]

Conversely, proposals to rescind approval of the NPV Interstate Compact have been introduced in the legislatures of Hawaii, Maryland, Massachusetts,

New Jersey, and Washington to date, but none has been approved.[110]

Following California's accession to the NPV compact in 2011, various conservative or libertarian groups announced measures to defend the electoral college system. On December 7, 2011, the Heritage Foundation hosted a forum at which guest speakers, including five state secretaries of state, expressed their concern over the National Popular Vote campaign.[111] On December 8 of the same year, Roll Call reported that the State Government Leadership Foundation, a project of the Republican State Leadership Committee, would begin a campaign to defend the electoral college and counter recent NPV gains.[112]

CONCLUDING OBSERVATIONS

The electoral college system emerged from the Philadelphia Convention of 1787 as one of the many compromises incorporated in the United States Constitution. It did not satisfy everyone, but it incorporated many of the goals sought for the presidential election process, including independence from control or influence by Congress, a substantial role for the states, and an effort to temper popular enthusiasms and partisan and sectional attachments by giving the actual vote to the electors, who, it was hoped, would be prominent citizens of their states and communities who would exercise restraint and balance in their choice of the President.

Since that time, it has been modified directly by the Twelfth and Twentieth Amendments to the Constitution and indirectly through the Fifteenth, Nineteenth, and Twenty-fifth Amendments, the passage of various federal and state laws, and changing political party practices and traditions. The electoral college functions today in a way that is far more democratic and political-party oriented than the founders might have anticipated or desired, but the three essential features of the system cited above remain intact: the process is largely free of structural interference by Congress; it is based strongly on federal principles; and the electors, although now all popularly elected, still make the final choice of the President an indirect one.

Despite the convention's satisfaction with its work, the electoral college has been criticized on various grounds from the earliest days under the republic; reform proposals were introduced in Congress as early as 1797.[113] Since that time, amendments have been introduced to reform or replace the electoral college with direct popular election in almost every session of Congress. Estimates vary, but they number at least 752 through the 115th Congress.[114]

For more than two decades in the mid-20th century, electoral college reform was actively considered in Congress. Relevant amendments were debated in the Senate on five occasions, and in the House, twice, but despite public support and the efforts of congressional leadership, none of these proposals met the stringent qualifications required by Article V of the Constitution: a two-thirds vote in both houses of Congress.

Congressional support and public interest in the question waned in the 21st century, notwithstanding an electoral college "misfire" in the presidential election of 2000, when, for the first time since 1888, a President was elected with a majority of electoral votes but fewer popular votes than his major-party opponent. During this period, the arena of electoral college reform was dominated for more than a decade by efforts at the state level, and by a non-governmental initiative, as noted earlier in this report. The states may continue to consider legislative action providing for changes in their procedures for allocating electoral votes by either the district or proportional systems. To date, however, such proposals have generated intense controversy and opposition in the states where they have been introduced, being regularly characterized by opponents as efforts to rig presidential elections and deprive minorities of their voting rights. To date, none has been successful. Barring unforeseen circumstances, such experiments do not appear to enjoy widespread support, and even if enacted, they might be subject to legal challenges on various grounds, including dilution of minority voter influence.

With respect to the National Popular Vote Initiative, despite its successful adoption by California in 2011 and New York in 2014, and the results of the 2016 election, the NPV interstate compact has yet to develop sustained momentum. While it has generated interest in various direct popular vote advocacy communities, it does not appear to have gained widespread awareness or support among the public at large.

Following the presidential election of 2016, congressional interest in reform, specifically direct popular election of the President and Vice President, revived; as noted previously, two measures are pending in the 115th Congress. To date, however, they have received no action beyond committee referral. These proposals face the exacting standards required by Article V of the Constitution, which establishes procedures for constitutional amendments. The founders intentionally made it difficult to revise the Constitution, establishing requirements for three separate super-majority votes: by two-thirds in both the Senate and House of Representatives Congress and ratification by three-quarters of the states. Congress exercises still further influence on the amendment process because it can choose ratification by state legislatures, or by ad hoc state ratification conventions, at its discretion. In practice, the standard for ratification is even higher, since it is customary to attach a seven-year deadline for ratification to all proposed amendments.

Notwithstanding sometimes vigorous advocacy in Congress, no electoral college reform amendment has been able to meet even the first step of this exacting requirement since the Twelfth Amendment in 1804. That measure, which responded to a fundamental constitutional crisis resulting from the deadlocked presidential election of 1800, led to an overwhelming consensus for reform. The Twelfth Amendment was debated and approved in Congress and ratified by the states within a span of six months, a remarkable achievement for the time. It is arguable that a contemporary electoral college reform amendment might require a comparable stimulus in order to succeed.

AUTHOR CONTACT INFORMATION

Thomas H. Neale Specialist in American National Government tneale@crs.loc.gov, 7-7883

1. According to the author, what are the key issues facing the Electoral College?

2. How have states addressed these issues in recent years?

EXCERPT FROM "WHO WILL BE THE NEXT PRESIDENT? A GUIDE TO THE U.S. PRESIDENTIAL ELECTION SYSTEM," BY ALEXANDER S. BELENKY, FROM *DSPACE@MIT*, 2013

CHAPTER 8

CONCLUSION: FUNDAMENTAL MERITS, EMBEDDED DEFICIENCIES, AND URGENT PROBLEMS OF THE U.S. PRESIDENTIAL ELECTION SYSTEM

The Conclusion briefly summarizes fundamental merits, substantial deficiencies, and certain problems of the currently existing U.S. presidential election system, which have been discussed in the book. Also, it outlines seven major topics relating to presidential elections on which public debates are likely to focus in the years to come: (a) what rules for electing a President and a Vice President are the fairest, (b) how to suppress voter fraud while not suppressing voter turnout; (c) how to improve the

Election Day procedures that affect the integrity of the election process; (d) how to broadcast polling results as election campaign develops to avoid "brainwashing" the voters and not to reduce the turnout, (e) what voting technologies can assure the American people that every vote cast is counted, (f) how to improve civics education relating to the election system to make every eligible voter interested in voting in presidential elections, and (g) who should govern the national televised presidential debates, and how these debates should be governed.

The U.S. presidential election system was proposed by the Constitutional Convention participants in Philadelphia in 1787. Its basic principles were set in Article 2 of the Constitution, but the proposed system was modified as a result of the Twelfth Amendment ratification in 1804. Since then, Amendments 20, 22, 23, and 25, which directly affect the structure and work of the presidential election system, and Amendments 13, 14, 15, 19, 24, and 26, which deal with the rights of American citizens to participate in all U.S. elections, including presidential ones, have been ratified. However, the basic principles of the system, set in Article 2 and Amendment 12, have practically remained unchanged.

The essence of these principles can be described as follows: Only the states and the District of Columbia (since 1964) rather than the American people can elect a U.S. President and a U.S. Vice President, and only the states have two attempts to elect these two executives. The first attempt is implemented by the states (and, since the 1964 presidential election, by the District of Columbia) via the Electoral College, which chooses both a President and a Vice President. Should this first attempt fail (and this happened twice, in the 1800 and in the 1824 elections), the second attempt to choose both executives is given to the states only. This second attempt is implemented via Congress, where the House of Representatives chooses a President, and the Senate chooses a Vice President.

Many constitutional scholars and specialists on the American history strongly believe that the Constitutional Convention participants (the Founding Fathers) attempted to create a republic of independent, equal states, rather than a democracy (as a form of governing the country). They believe that the Founding Fathers wanted to avoid the "tyranny of majority" and to provide the independence and balance of all the three branches of authorities in the country—executive, legislative, and judicial—particularly, by rejecting the idea of direct presidential elections by the American people. Some of these scholars and specialists believe that the Founding Fathers were sure that a mandate from the nation to the Chief Executive, on who the Constitution vests all the executive power in the country, would give this branch of the country's authorities a more weight in governing the country than each of the other two branches would have.

8.1 FUNDAMENTAL MERITS OF THE SYSTEM

A brief summary of the fundamental merits of the existing U.S. presidential election system to follow should be viewed as the author's attempt to analyze to what extent the existing system corresponds to underlying basic ideas and principles reflected in the Constitution and in the Supreme Court decisions relating to U.S. presidential elections. All the reasoning presented in the text does not reflect any emotional perceptions of this election system that American voters and residents may have.

1. In the absence of national and international disasters, the work of the U.S. presidential election system always ends on Inauguration Day. Either an elected President or a person from a set of eligible persons is assigned President and is sworn in by taking the oath. This set includes the list of eligible persons determined by a document adopted by Congress in line with the requirements of the Twentieth Amendment. Currently, the Presidential Succession Act of 1947 is this document (though its constitutionality is questioned by some prominent constitutional scholars). This act (a) has done away with the Presidential Succession Act of 1886, and (b) has reinstated the order of the first two people on the list that existed in the initial Presidential Succession Act of 1792. The state legislature from each of the fifty states and that from the District of Columbia appoint state and D.C. presidential electors, respectively. The appointed electors are to vote for President and for Vice President on the same day in the places of their residence (states and D.C.). Both state and DC legislatures are free to choose a manner of appointing electors within their jurisdictions. Currently, presidential electors are appointed by holding popular elections in each of the states and in D.C., and the Constitution does not permit

(a) any repetition of voting to detect the will of the states or D.C. in electing state or D.C. electors to the Electoral College, and

(b) any repetition of voting to detect the will of elected (or appointed) electors (i.e. the Electoral College members from the states and from the District of Columbia).

2. The act of electing or appointing a President does not depend on the number of voters who may decide to vote for electors in the states of their residence and in D.C. Even if all the state eligible voters from any state (or eligible voters from D.C.) decide (a) not to vote for presidential electors at all, or (b) to vote against all the slates of the state (and D.C.) electors, the electors who are to represent the states (and D.C.) in the Electoral College will be appointed by the state and D.C. That is, Article 2 of the Constitution obliges every state to appoint state electors to the Electoral College in line with the manner of appointing state electors determined by the state legislature. Analogously, Amendment 23 of the Constitution obliges the District of Columbia to appoint its presidential electors to the Electoral College in line with the manner of appointing presidential electors determined by Congress for D.C. (In 1973, however, Congress officially transferred this authority to the administration of the District of Columbia.) The Constitution obliges all the electors to vote in their respective states and in the District of Columbia on the same day, which is currently the first Monday after the second Wednesday of December of the election year.

3. Making changes to the presidential election system that go beyond the authority of the states can be done only in the form of amendments to the Constitution. A

proposal to consider a constitutional amendment is to be approved by either a two-third majority of votes cast in each of the two Chambers of Congress or by a special Convention that Congress may call for at the request of state legislatures from a two-third majority of all the states. To become part of the Constitution, every thus-approved amendment is to be ratified by either the state legislature in each of any three-fourths of all the states or by state Conventions called for in each of any three-fourths of all the states.

4. Any intermediate results of the work of the presidential election system can be challenged only in court (as happened, for instance, in the course of the 2000 election, when the voting results in the state of Florida regarding the composition of the state electors to represent the state in the Electoral College were challenged).

5. Each state and the District of Columbia can change the manner of appointing their presidential electors independently of the other states.

From the author's viewpoint, the listed merits of the system are fundamental, make this system unique, and may explain why this system has been in use from more than 220 years.

8.2 EMBEDDED DEFICIENCIES OF THE SYSTEM

The following description of substantial deficiencies of the presidential election system takes into consideration only

(a) provisions of the Constitution relating to the presidential election system, and (b) the Supreme Court rulings that explicitly determine how one should understand these provisions. It is these provisions and rulings rather than any

- opinions of the Supreme Court judges that are expressed in the course of discussing any constitutional matters,
- interpretations of both constitutional provisions and the above-mentioned opinions by constitutional scholars, and
- numerical estimates of the chances of weird, undesirable, and extreme situations to emerge in the course of presidential elections

that constitute the basis for this description. Certainly, the system has other deficiencies; however, those under consideration in this paragraph are the deficiencies embedded in the Constitution that may eventually cause the intervention of the Supreme Court in the election process.

1. Constitutionally, presidential electors are free agents, i.e., they are free to make their decisions in voting for both a President and a Vice President. The Constitution does not limit any elector (i.e., any member of the Electoral College) in her/his decision to vote in the Electoral College. That is, each elector can (a) vote for any two persons (for one as President and for the other as Vice President), (b) cast one of the ballots or even both ballots blank, or (c) cast the ballots that cannot be recognized as votes favoring any person. This state of affairs takes place despite the fact that

- every elector from a state or from the District of Columbia belongs to a slate of electors submitted by the pair of presidential and vice-presidential candidates heading this slate in the state and in the District of Columbia, as well as in each congressional district of the states of Maine and Nebraska, and

- it is assumed that every member of the Electoral College (elector) from every state and from the District of Columbia will vote in favor of the pair of the candidates whose slate of electors (a) won in this state, in the District of Columbia, and in congressional districts of the states of Maine and Nebraska, respectively, and (b) contains the name of this elector.

Moreover, the above-mentioned two persons do not need to be either presidential or vice-presidential candidates in the election year.

Currently, election laws in 21 of 50 states do not oblige a state elector to favor presidential and vice-presidential candidates who head the slate of electors that (a) is to represent the state in the Electoral College, and (b) contains the name of this elector. (These 21 states currently control 208 out of 538 electoral votes in the Electoral College.) Five of the other 29 states have election laws punishing faithless electors. However, the constitutionality of these laws has never been challenged, and these laws have never been put to a test. Even under these laws, the elector may be punished only after she/he has cast the vote in the Electoral College. So, generally, these laws may not affect the elector's decision. In 2008, two states from the 29 states passed election laws that allow these states to nullify votes of faithless electors. However, the constitutionality of these laws has never been put to a test either.

The Supreme Court has never ruled that an elector must vote in line with the will of the state which this elector represents in the Electoral College. Yet different opinions on this matter have been expressed by the Supreme Court members in the course of considering various constitutional issues.

Examples of faithlessly cast votes by electors in the Electoral College are well known (see, for instance, Chap. 2 and the books [4, 6, 8]).

Thus, constitutionally, results of voting of more than 200 million eligible voters in the country and those of voting in the Electoral College in an election year may not necessarily coincide.

As mentioned earlier (see Sect. 2.2), theoretically, if for whatever reasons, all the appointed presidential electors vote faithlessly (by casting ballots that cannot be recognized as votes favoring presidential and vice-presidential candidates), the only provision to complete the election would then be the Twelfth Amendment, provided the Supreme Court confirmed that "the Vice President," mentioned in the amendment, is the sitting one and attributed (only) definition (b) (see Chap. 3) to the verb "to qualify" from the Twentieth Amendment.

2. The text of the Twelfth Amendment leaves it unclear how many persons (two or three) should be voted for as President in an election of a President thrown into the House or Representatives, when (a) at least three persons have received electoral votes as President in the Electoral College, and (b) none of these persons has received a majority of votes of all the appointed electors as President in the Electoral College. Indeed, according to the Twelfth Amendment, no more than three persons rather than two or three persons exactly can be voted for as President in the House of Representatives in an election of a President thrown into Congress.

3. The text of the Twelfth Amendment leaves it unclear how two persons who are to be voted for as Vice President in an election of a Vice President thrown into the Senate, should be selected when (a) none of the electoral vote recipients has received a majority of the votes of all the appointed electors in the Electoral College as Vice President, and (b) at least three persons voted for as Vice President in the Electoral College have received one and the same greatest number of votes.

From the author's viewpoint, these embedded deficiencies make the U.S. presidential election system vulnerable and dependent on decisions of particular individuals rather than dependent only on constitutional provisions and legislations of Congress authorized by these provisions.

8.3 SOME URGENT PROBLEMS OF THE SYSTEM

A brief description of some urgent problems of the existing presidential election system is based on the analysis of opinions on this system expressed by some political leaders, American voters, journalists, commentators, etc. These opinions do not reflect to what extent this system is in line with its underlying ideas and principles reflected in the Constitution and with the Supreme Court decisions on matters relating to presidential elections.

1. The U.S. presidential election system is quite complicated to understand all its details in depth. Despite this system being studied in American schools, a sizable number of American voters are convinced that on Election Day—i.e., on the first Tuesday next after the first Monday in the month of November of the election year—they vote for President and for Vice President. Since only the names of pairs of presidential and vice-presidential candidates heading the slates of state and D. C. electors appear on the (short) ballots, many voters do not know that they do not vote for these pairs of presidential and vice-presidential candidates. American voters vote in their respective states and in the District of Columbia only for the slates of electors submitted by the pairs of presidential and vice-presidential candidates who compete in the states (and in D.C.), as well as in each congressional district of the states of Maine and Nebraska. Moreover, constitutionally, even this limited participation of voters in every

state in electing presidential electors fully depends on the will of the state legislature. The Constitution allows the state legislature of every state to appoint all state electors in the Electoral College by themselves, without holding any election for these electors in the state. Many Americans do not understand that the presidential election system can cause election outcomes undesirable to them, and the election result of the 2000 presidential election in Florida seems to illustrate this.

2. As mentioned earlier, since 1824, there exists a tradition of counting "votes of all the voting voters" received by (the electors of) presidential candidates in all the states (and since the 1964 election, in the District of Columbia as well). The tally of all these votes, which does not have any legitimacy, is called the "national popular vote." This tally has this name despite the fact that, formally, it is a sum of the votes cast by eligible voters in different states and in D. C. for different slates of electors. Four times—in 1824, 1876, 1888, and 2000—the Electoral College elected President those presidential candidates who did not win the tallied national popular vote. Each time, this discrepancy was negatively received by the American people.

Available poll results bear evidence that an overwhelming majority of the respondents believe that a President should be elected in direct popular elections by American voters rather than by the Electoral College. However, all the attempts to initiate a constitutional amendment to change the existing presidential election system have so far failed.

3. In the framework of the existing election system, votes of the voting voters have the same weight in determining the voting results only within a state and within the District of Columbia. This causes discontent among a sizable number of American voters, who believe that Presidents should be elected according to the principle "one person, one vote." It is this principle that is in use in all the American elections, except for presidential ones.

4. The deployment of the "winner-take-all" principle by state legislatures in 48 states and in the District of Columbia in electing presidential electors causes election campaigns of the major party candidates to focus on a few (10–15) so-called "battleground" or 'swing" states. In each of these "swing" states, the number of votes supporting pairs of presidential and vice-presidential candidates from two major political parties turns out to have been close (or even almost the same) for the last 20–30 years. In each of the other so-called "safe" states— many of which are densely populous ones, such as California, Texas, New York, and Florida—an overwhelming majority of all the voting voters usually prefer the candidates from one of the two major political parties in all the elections (except for, maybe, elections of the governors). In the framework of the "winner-take-all" principle, presidential candidates do not have any reason to actively campaign in the densely populous states. Such a tendency causes a great deal of discontent in many American voters from these "safe" populous states. Many of them strongly believe that presidential elections should

be held according to the principle "one person, one vote" in the framework of direct popular elections.

The author believes these problems to be urgent, since their presence in the system affects the confidence of American voters on the fairness of the U.S. presidential election system.

8.4 SEVEN MAJOR TOPICS RELATING TO PRESIDENTIAL ELECTIONS

In recent years American society has become deeply divided about whether the current election system is fair and serves the country well. Those who believe that it is and does, do not even say that the U.S. cannot talk about how democratic national elections are in other countries as long as its own presidential election system does not serve the popular will.

Many Americans support the idea to do away with the Electoral College and elect presidents by popular vote, whereas others strongly oppose such a move and assert that it would weaken the federal structure of government. The accuracy of counting the votes cast remains in question for a sizable part of the electorate. Some voters believe that partisan authorities may artificially design voter queues to deter voters from voting in places in which support of their political opponents is substantial. There is no consensus on whether presenting a voter ID at a polling station should be a must, and whether convicted felons should retain the right to vote. Finally, American society is becoming more and more concerned regarding the influence that numerous pre-election polls, sponsored by the media, may have on the voter turnout and election outcomes.

Strengthening the confidence of the American people in institutions of the U.S. democracy and encouraging eligible voters to exercise their right to vote are a challenge. As mentioned earlier in this book (see Chap. 7), the existing presidential election system is not easy to understand in depth, which leaves many eligible voters unaware of the value of their vote in presidential elections. An unsatisfactory civics education of both today's and future voters makes them vulnerable to both partisan political manipulation and ideological propaganda.

The American people, have both the right and the obligation to know how the existing presidential election system serves the nation so that they can decide (a) whether the whole system or any part of it should be replaced with other election mechanisms, and (b) what can be done within the existing system to address the above issues.

Public debates on the following seven major topics relating to the election system are long overdue: (a) The Electoral College v. the National Popular Vote plan and other plans to improve the current election system; (b) voter identification: how to suppress voter fraud while not suppressing voter turnout; (c) Election Day procedures and the integrity of the election process; (d) polling and elections: whether society is informed or "brainwashed" by the media regarding how election campaigns really develop; (e) voting technologies: how far the technologies have advanced since the 2000 Florida election in making the American people sure that every vote cast is counted; (f) civics education: what Americans know, and what they do not know about the election system that makes more than 40 % of all eligible voters not interested in participating even in presidential elections, and (g) who should govern the national televised presidential debates, and how these debates should be governed.

Though some of these topics have been addressed in surveys regarding the election system, for instance, in [78–80], as well as in numerous publications on the related issues, for instance, in [81], American society remains polarized regarding these issues, and further studies of the issues within the topics are needed. The following studies in each of the issues seem urgent:

The Electoral College. Since the 2000 election, a sizable part of society has shared the belief that a person who has received the most votes should be President. In contrast, many voters and residents continue to believe that despite all the controversies whirling around the current system, this system best reflects the preferences of the states, which is the underlying idea of the Electoral College. The emergence of the National Popular Vote (NPV) movement, aimed at changing the current election system without amending the Constitution, its strong support by a part of society, and an equally strong rejection of the NPV idea by another part of society bear evidence that both above-mentioned beliefs have grounds and cannot be ignored any longer.

The originators and proponents of the National Popular Vote plan for changing the current election system interpret the provision of Article 2 of the Constitution favorable to their cause. That is, they assert that a compact formed by the states controlling at least 270 electoral votes combined can collectively decide who should be the next President, no matter what the rest of the country decides [5]. Certainly, this interpretation of the above constitutional provision is no more than a particular belief of a group of people, and it cannot be declared true or false until supported or rejected by the Supreme Court, as in the case with any constitutional matter.

However, this interpretation has already become a public policy currently in ten states—Maryland, New Jersey, New York, Illinois, Rhode Island, Massachusetts, California, Vermont, Hawaii, Washington—and in the District of Columbia, (currently) accounting for 165 electoral votes.

Opponents of the plan assert that not only does this plan violate the Constitution, in particular, the Equal Protection Clause from the Fourteenth Amendment, but that the NPV plan promises to the voters something that it cannot deliver—the equal interest of all the presidential candidates in campaigning in all the states [1].

The originators and proponents of the NPV plan blame the "winner-take-all" method for awarding state electoral votes for dividing the country into "safe" and "battleground" states and localizing the election campaign only in the "battlegrounds." Yet this plan is based on methods like "winner-take-all" in which a voter in a state cannot vote for electors from different slates of state electors.

The opponents of the NPV plan suggest that under the plan, the country will be divided into "battleground" densely populated metropolitan areas, where most voting voters reside, and rural, sparsely populated areas. They suggest that voting voters in rural areas constitute a small percentage of all voting voters and can be ignored by the candidates in any presidential elections, except for extremely close ones, rare for large electorates. Moreover, they suggest approaches to changing the system to treat the small- and medium-size states more fairly, which is likely to encourage presidential candidates to campaign in small states [1, 18, 22].

Should any group of states opposing the NPV plan decide to use methods for awarding state electoral votes other than the "winner-take-all," the "tally" of votes cast for electors of presidential candidates will no longer represent the popular will. The electoral votes that the compact of states would award according to the above "tally" under the NPV rules could no longer be viewed as those awarded on behalf of the whole country [1, 33, 58].

Without consensus in society on the NPV plan, and without a decision on its constitutionality by the Supreme Court, it may happen that only the state-signatories to the NPV compact will be contributors to the "tally" of votes cast for slates of presidential electors. If this were the case, the country would become divided into the states that would insist on following the current election rules, which could favor candidate A, and the state-signatories to the NPV compact, which would declare candidate B the election winner [33, 58].

The issue of changing the current election system in any manner should become a subject of public discussion, and possibly, a referendum, where the American people can vote on any plan offered as a replacement for the current system.

Voter Identification. Voter ID laws that some states have already instituted and some states would like to institute are a public policy concerning the integrity of the election process. Currently, there is no consensus in society on whether any such laws should be passed. Some prominent lawmakers, public figures, journalists, and voters believe that election fraud cannot be avoided unless every voter is required to present an ID at the polling station. Some others believe that this requirement is unnecessary due to an insufficient amount of fraud caused by the absence of voter IDs, whereas its enforcement will suppress voter turnout, especially that of minorities and elderly voters [82, 83].

Voter ID laws are not federal but state public policies, and these policies vary across the states. According to the National Conference of State Legislatures [83], currently, seventeen states (Georgia, Indiana, Kansas, Mississippi, North Dakota, Tennessee, Virginia, Texas, Wisconsin, Alabama, Florida, Hawaii, Idaho, Louisiana, Michigan, Rhode Island, and South Dakota) require a photo ID, whereas another 16 states (Arizona, Ohio, Alaska, Arkansas, Colorado, Connecticut, Delaware, Kentucky, Missouri, Montana, New Hampshire, North Carolina, Oklahoma, South Carolina, Utah, and Washington) require some form of a non-photo ID or its alternatives at the polling stations. Among the above seventeen states, nine states (Georgia, Indiana, Kansas, Mississippi, North Dakota, Tennessee, Virginia, Texas, and Wisconsin) allow the voters who fail to provide a voter ID to vote on a provisional ballot (though such an ID is required by the state law). However, these voters must provide an acceptable form of ID later on (within a few days after the election) to have their provisional ballots counted. In the other eight states (Alabama, Florida, Hawaii, Idaho, Louisiana, Michigan, Rhode Island, and South Dakota), the voter without an ID is allowed to cast a provisional ballot if either this voter signs a certain paper (for instance, the affidavit of identity) or a poll worker vouches for the voter. In any case, the eligibility of the voter is verified though no action from the voter is required.

At the same time, cases challenging both the status quo and the attempts to block voter ID laws are pending in several states.

There are conservative groups in the country that claim to have witnessed the registration of sizable numbers of ineligible and even non-existent voters, whereas there are liberal groups who claim that the voter fraud has never been sufficient enough to pass voter ID laws in the first place. Thus, the right of eligible citizens to vote in any election should not be compromised by any state laws, and the right of all eligible voters to have only legitimately cast votes counted should not be compromised either.

Election Day Procedures. Voting queues are another issue relating to the integrity of the election process, especially in federal elections, which constitutionally are conducted under different state laws.

Voter queues in presidential elections drew national attention when the 2000 and 2004 nail-biter elections warned American society that the queues might have affected the outcomes of both elections. Published studies suggest that, in the recent elections, long lines have contributed to discouraging from voting up to 2 % of all eligible voters, which could have made a difference in close elections in particular "battleground" states. However, the voter queue problem, most recently actively discussed in the country during the 2008 election, does not seem to have stirred much interest.

In the 2000 election, George W. Bush won the presidency by a margin of just 537 votes in Florida. Thus, if at least 538 Floridians who came to the precincts did not have a chance to vote due to the widely reported long lines, one cannot be certain regarding the fairness of the election outcome [84].

In the 2004 election, fewer than 119,000 Ohio votes might have decided the election outcome. Bipartisan accounts suggest that in Columbus, an average of 21 would-be voters per precinct were discouraged by reported waits of up to fourteen hours. Simple arithmetic suggests that if this rate of discouragement held in all 12 of the most populated Ohio counties, with 6560 precincts—where official tallies showed John Kerry won a majority of votes—the election result might have been different [84, 85].

Election queues mostly form when the number of voting machines and support personnel are insufficient to handle swiftly the voters entering the polling station. Culprits include statistical underestimation, incompetence, equipment malfunction, and voter inexperience, especially in dealing with new machines. However, a deliberate manipulation may also be a factor [85].

Certain voting precincts can be intentionally "understaffed" with voting machines and personnel. Creating queues can be a potent weapon of partisan election authorities for suppressing voters believed to favor the other party. Among possible abuses that compromise elections, this tactic is difficult to detect, much less to prove. As there are no "exit polls" of voters who gave up because of long lines, red flags are not raised, and stealth disenfranchisement is a real possibility [86].

Malfunctions of voting equipment in the 2000 presidential election led to the Help America Vote Act (HAVA), passed by Congress in 2002 [87]. In contrast, the deployment of voting machines still does not have any federal oversight [85].

Service science suggests that establishing and enforcing voting standards, such as the maximum wait time to cast a vote, is the key to avoiding long lines on Election Day. Making a maximum waiting period a federal standard would provide "accessibility equity" for all voters [88].

The absence of reasonable voting standards is a double-edged sword. Partisan election administrators can artificially design voter queues in particular precincts to discourage would-be voters favoring their political opponents. Election administrators interested in fairly conducting elections do not have grounds to substantiate their requests for state or federal funds to meet even minimum expectations of voting voters (assuming that the administrators know how to meet them).

Polling and Elections. Predicting the outcomes of American presidential elections has become a business of the media with millions of customers both in the U.S. and around the world. While the predictions as such are undoubtedly entertaining, they affect the decisions of voters receptive to the opinions of political pundits, journalists, hosts of radio and TV talk shows, etc. Also, the prediction of the election outcome may affect the campaigns of presidential candidates due to changing the mood of potential financial donors to contribute to the "war chests" of particular candidates. The closer the election, the more attentive are the world financial markets to the predictions [89]. There are well-studied bandwagon and underdog effects of election outcome predictions [6, 80], which suggest that predictions of presidential election outcomes are a powerful weapon capable of affecting these outcomes.

The most important effect the predictions of presidential election outcomes have is that on voter turnout, discouraging from voting those voters who trust the predictions both favorable and unfavorable to their favorites, no matter whether these predictions are trustworthy or misleading. However, despite the obvious impact of the outcome predictions on the voter turnout, the problem has never been studied in depth.

Voting technologies. Voting technologies, especially voting machines, have been a focus of society since the 2000 election. Several studies, including those conducted in the framework of the CALTECH-MIT project, have been done, and research in the field continues.

From the CALTECH-MIT project, some conclusions have been drawn on what impact voting technologies have had on the so-called residual ballots, i.e., blank, overvoted, and undervoted ballots, and several security issues associated with the use of electronic voting machines have been identified and studied. A summary of some of these studies has been presented in several surveys, for instance, in [90, 91].

Obviously, the accuracy of counting the votes by voting machines remains among the major issues affecting the integrity of the election issues and the quality of the whole election system.

Civics Education: Civic studies of the presidential election system are mandatory in American schools.

Yet future voters study this subject superficially, without understanding the principles underlying the current election system, which the Founding Fathers embedded in the Constitution. Nor do they understand the value of votes cast by voting voters in the election under any particular rules of determining the election winner, including the Electoral College ones [92, 93].

The basic rules for determining an election winner should be surveyed and discussed, and educational materials on the subject, including those currently available on the Internet [94], should become part of civics education. Also, discussing various voting rules will offer a comparative analysis of the pros and cons of these rules, as well as an analysis of the perspectives on their use in U.S. federal elections, including presidential elections.

National Televised Presidential Debates. According to the available data [95], in 2012, there were 30,700,138 members of the Republican Party and 43,140,758 members of the Democratic Party. Among the 129,237,642 voting voters in the 2012 presidential election, 1,108,805 voters favored minor-party candidates [31]. Thus, even if all the members of both major parties voted in the 2012 election, about 54 million voting voters were independents. This number greatly exceeds the number of members of either major party at that time. This simple arithmetic seems to be in line with the Gallup Poll results of January 11, 2016, which show that 42 % of American adults consider themselves independents [96].

Yet one may argue that no matter how many voters call themselves independents, together, two major-party presidential candidates usually receive more than 95 % of all the votes cast. In the 1992 and 1996 elections, however, they received less than 81 and 91 %, respectively [31], but these two elections were an exception. The participation of a strong independent candidate in the national televised presidential debates in the 1992 election substantially affected that election outcome. At the same time, his absence from the national televised debates in 1996 (though as a candidate from the Reform Party in that election), apparently, contributed to a substantial drop in his popularity on Election Day.

The Commission on Presidential Debates (CPD)—a private, non-profit organization formed in 1987—has had a monopoly on holding presidential debates since the 1988 election. Soon after the Commission was formed, the League of Women Voters decided to quit sponsoring these debates. This happened once it became known that the election campaigns of the two major party candidates had reached a secret agreement on how the debates should be held and ruled [97].

Neither the Constitution nor any federal statutes regulate these debates. The Federal Election Commission (FEC) regulations allow any 501(c)(3) and (c)(4) tax-exempt organization to hold federal candidate debates if it does not endorse or oppose political candidates or parties. The only requirement to be a "staging organization" for these debates is "to follow pre-established criteria on which candidates may participate in the debates" and not to use the "nomination by a particular political party as the sole objective criterion to determine whether to include a candidate in a debate" [98].

The CPD rules require persons interested in participating in the national televised presidential debates (a) to achieve at least 15 % of the popular support on national polls conducted by "five selected national public opinion polling organizations," and (b) to be constitutionally eligible to the office of President and to be on the ballot in states controlling at least 270 electoral votes combined [99, 100].

Nobody knows which particular polls should be trusted and (why), when the support is to be demonstrated (and for how long), and whether all the presidential nominees are in the question of the top line. As egregious as this may seem, in the most developed democracy in the world, the CPD, a private firm, is free to dictate its fuzzy rules for presidential debates—a matter of national importance.

The historical "jump" of Ross Perot from 8 % of the popular support before the televised debates to almost 19 % on Election Day 1992 suggests that with respect to non-major party candidates, the CPD rules are a "Catch 22" [99]. Without gaining publicity via televised debates with major party candidates, a non-major party candidate is unlikely to achieve 15 % of the public support. Yet without this support, the CPD does not let the candidate into these debates.

While the CPD claims to be non-partisan towards either major party, its rules look completely partisan towards all the other political parties and independent candidates combined. Due to the CPD rules, in presidential elections, the American people are, in fact, forced to choose only between two major-party nominees, even if unfavorable ratings of either nominee exceed 50 %, which seems to be the case in the 2016 presidential election [101].

Thus, these rules leave more than 40 % of independent voters underrepresented in presidential debates, as well as in presidential elections.

In the CPD televised presidential debates, both major-party candidates only name problems that concern Americans and promise to take care of them if elected. They can afford to do this since the non-major party candidates, willing to discuss these problems, are cut off from the debates even in the primary season. Nobody knows whether the promises made are trustworthy and even implementable (particularly, financially) since no solutions and calculations are offered. The debaters focus on personal attacks on their opponents and go after them on private matters.

The CPD debates look like cage fights. Agile and wily debaters win by personally harming their opponents, or making fun of them, or both. Particular issues, that lovely word of the candidates who often have no clue on how to deal with them in reality, are not discussed as deeply as they deserve. Nor are they often even mentioned. Instead of a competition of ideas, the debates offer only a comparison of candidate disadvantages.

Is this good for America?

The country can only lose by electing a President out of two candidates whose plans for the country have not been discussed in depth in front of interested voters and experts. The CDP discriminatory debate rules contribute to distorting the real preferences of the American people. If non-major party candidates participated in TV presidential debates, many independent voters would probably still favor major-party candidates. However, their choice would then be free rather than being affected by the CDP rules.

Can the non-major parties and independent voters change this status quo? Yes, they can.

The CPD would certainly change the debate rules if a strong competing force came into play, as usually happens in any private business.

Alternative TV debates and/or online debates are likely to draw the attention of both the American voters and all the presidential candidates, including the two major-party ones, especially if experts offer their opinions as well.

Three challenges associated with organizing and holding such alternative debates should be addressed.

First, the cost of technically communicating the debates to, for instance, the Internet audience, which will be much lower than that of the TV ones, needs to be covered. One should estimate the numbers and explore the sources of the coverage. Any alternative and/or online presidential debate staging organizations are to be allowed by the FEC to accept funds from labor unions and corporations to "defray costs incurred in staging candidate debates" [98]. Certainly, foundations caring about the election fairness should be allowed to sponsor such debates.

Though businesses will undoubtedly be glad to use this unique opportunity to advertize their products to millions of debate viewers, their contributions should be approved by the FEC in some form. The same is true for possible small private contributions from the inter-ested audience, and the grass-root financing of Senator Bernie Sanders' 2016 campaign bears evidence that there is room for this.

Second, the alternative TV and/or online debates should be run completely differently from the CPD "shows" that are currently offered in the TV debates. Though there still may be certain reasonable thresholds to overcome to be eligible to participate in the debates [102], both established political parties and independent presidential candidates should be able to participate. Criteria to consider candidates established should be set by experts and approved by the American people rather than being arbitrarily set by the CPD.

To be considered established, a non-major party presidential candidate or an independent one should demonstrate a certain level of public support, both locally and nationwide, to appear on TV programs, radio talk shows, etc., i.e., become noticeable in the public arena. It is possible that several such established candidates would first need to debate among themselves on the Internet, on TV and radio programs, and in the state and national newspapers. All interested persons can start these activities well in advance of the presidential election season, and the activity results will reflect public interest in their ideas and programs. This interest, measured by the level of the public support attained, will either let or not let them overcome the thresholds to be allowed to compete with the major-party candidates in any national televised presidential debates. The experience of running such debates for non-major party candidates and for the "newcomers" has long existed in Europe, and this experience may be helpful.

Once the set of presidential candidates from non-major parties and independent ones to be on the alternative TV and/or online debates has been determined, a list of issues to be discussed at the debates should be suggested by the potential viewers. Each debate should cover a particular issue or a group of connected issues from the list. The candidates should understand that they would be better off to be aware of the specifics of the issues which are the subject of each debate, since they are to argue with each other and also with invited recognized experts in the field. These experts will explain to the audience in a simple manner whether each candidate's proposal is implementable, will not harm the American economy and/or security, and will not make problems even more complicated. As a result of these debates, all interested Americans will see who of the candidates (a) shares their values, (b) is the most capable of solving problems that concern today's America, (c) is more knowledgeable, and (d) the best prepared to run the country.

Third, the alternative TV and/or online debates should be organized in such a manner that the candidates from both major political parties would not refuse to participate in them. Currently, the Internet reaches tens of millions of American voters, and presidential candidates need to earn their support by Election Day. In the era of television dominance, presidential candidates could afford to ignore their non-major party opponents [103, 104]. Particularly, with online debates, no candidate will dare to refuse to debate and let the opponents take advantage of her/his refusal to reach millions of voters. Also, deep concerns of many Americans about the future of the country and their distrust for both the legislative and the executive branches of the government have reached a critical level, as the 2016 election campaign has demonstrated. At this state of affairs, one cannot any longer deprive concerned voters either from substantive debates on real problems that they face in their everyday lives or from seeing alternatives to both major parties. Any refusal to participate in substantive debates with non-major party candidates and experts may cost the major-party candidates a defeat in the election.

Alternative TV and/or online substantive presidential debates will not exclude the CPD debates but will help Americans see who best can solve the country's problems. The CPD debates should let the candidates demonstrate their ability to react quickly, look presidential, and lead. The alternative TV and/or online debates should let the voters judge which candidate understands their problems better and more deeply. However, making the debates of both types inseparable will keep any debate staging organizations from excluding established non-major party candidates and independents from the debates.

Certainly, the idea of running alternative TV and/or online presidential debates will likely engender a great deal of criticism, especially from the conservatives, since they may believe that such debates are a threat to the existing two-party political system. However, this could be the case only if both major parties veer far away from voter expectations. On the contrary, holding such debates may produce an outcome desirable to both major parties. That is, if the major-party candidates come to the debates better prepared and more convincing than all their opponents, they may gain party supporters and even new members for their parties.

In any case, presidential candidates from established non-major political parties and independents who have overcome the above-mentioned thresholds should not be deprived from participating in televised presidential debates by artificially imposed unreasonable discriminatory requirements that are impossible to meet. Nor should the voters be left by the major parties to choose a President exceptionally based upon the financial capabilities of these parties rather than on the merits of all the presidential nominees.

Alternative TV and/or online debates that allow the nominees of established non-major party candidates to participate will make every presidential election more accurately reflect the will of the people. All the people.

Finally, supporters of the two-party system may argue that alternative TV and/or online presidential debates will "siphon" votes from major party candidates and will likely throw the election into Congress. Even if this is the case, at least currently, the two-party House of Representatives will unlikely elect a President other than from a major party though it may produce a President who has lost both the popular vote and the electoral vote.

Also, it seems reasonable to remind the conservatives that throwing a particular presidential election into Congress and electing a President in the House of Representatives is part of the existing presidential election system. Moreover, as mentioned in Sect. 1.5, in designing this system, the Founding Fathers may not have expected the Electoral College to always elect a President. According to their vision, if the Electoral College failed, the final say would belong to the states as equal members of the Union. The Founding Fathers considered the Electoral College failure a result of the lack of consensus among the electors, particularly, due to the difference in their opinions on who is the best to fill the office of President. Under today's presidential election system, the same lack of consensus among American voters on who is the best to be President may lead to the same failure of the Electoral College to produce a President.

If the voters know how the existing U.S. presidential election system works, they will likely make the right choice, being aware of the consequences of their vote. The author hopes that both the outlined seven topics to be discussed in the course of election campaigns and the present guide to the U.S. presidential election system may help American voters make this right choice on Election Day.

1. What is a "winner-take-all" approach to the Electoral College? Is it controversial? Why or why not?

2. How do other issues identified by the author interact with the Electoral College?

CHAPTER 2

WHAT POLITICIANS SAY

The role of politicians in the Electoral College can be obscure. Presidents, as a norm, do not comment extensively on the validity of the Electoral College, as doing so can be seen as interference in the election process. Congressional representatives from their parties, however, are free to discuss the Electoral College—and in recent years, some have moved to reform the process. But the political posturing around the Electoral College, particularly following elections with contentious results, can obscure the fact that the debate about the College's role in elections has been highly fraught for years. This can also tarnish the way we understand specific acts of Congress to change or otherwise introduce reforms to the process.

"A JOINT RESOLUTION PROPOSING AN AMENDMENT TO THE CONSTITUTION OF THE UNITED STATES TO ABOLISH THE ELECTORAL COLLEGE AND TO PROVIDE FOR THE DIRECT POPULAR ELECTION OF THE PRESIDENT AND VICE PRESIDENT OF THE UNITED STATES," SPONSORED BY SENATOR BARBARA BOXER, FROM THE SENATE, NOVEMBER 15, 2016

S. J. RES. 41

Proposing an amendment to the Constitution of the United States to abolish the electoral college and to provide for the direct popular election of the President and Vice President of the United States.

IN THE SENATE OF THE UNITED STATES

NOVEMBER 15, 2016

Mrs. Boxer (for herself and Mrs. Feinstein) introduced the following joint resolution; which was read twice and referred to the Committee on the Judiciary

JOINT RESOLUTION

Proposing an amendment to the Constitution of the United States to abolish the electoral college and to provide for the direct popular election of the President and Vice President of the United States.

Resolved by the Senate and House of Representatives of the United States of America in Congress assembled (two-thirds of each House concurring therein), That the following article is proposed as an amendment to the Constitution of the United States, which shall be valid to all intents and purposes as part of the Constitution when ratified by the legislatures of three-fourths of the several States within seven years after the date of its submission by the Congress:

"Article —

"SECTION 1. The President and Vice President shall be jointly elected by the direct vote of the qualified electors of the several States and territories and the District constituting the seat of Government of the United States. The electors in each State, territory, and the District constituting the seat of Government of the United States shall have the qualifications requisite for electors of the most numerous branch of the legislative body where they reside.

"SECTION 2. Congress may determine the time, place, and manner of holding the election, the entitlement to inclusion on the ballot, and the manner in which the results of the election shall be ascertained and declared."

1. How does a direct vote differ from the Electoral College system?

2. Do you think such a bill would ever be passed? Why or why not?

"H.CON.RES.79 - EXPRESSING THE SENSE OF CONGRESS THAT CONGRESS AND THE STATES SHOULD CONSIDER A CONSTITUTIONAL AMENDMENT TO REFORM THE ELECTORAL COLLEGE AND ESTABLISH A PROCESS FOR ELECTING THE PRESIDENT AND VICE PRESIDENT BY A NATIONAL POPULAR VOTE AND SHOULD ENCOURAGE INDIVIDUAL STATES TO CONTINUE TO REFORM THE ELECTORAL COLLEGE PROCESS THROUGH SUCH STEPS AS THE FORMATION OF AN INTERSTATE COMPACT TO AWARD THE MAJORITY OF ELECTORAL COLLEGE VOTES TO THE NATIONAL POPULAR VOTE WINNER," SPONSORED BY REPRESENTATIVE JOHN CONVERS, JR., FROM THE HOUSE OF REPRESENTATIVES, SEPTEMBER 14, 2017

H. CON. RES. 79

Expressing the sense of Congress that Congress and the States should consider a constitutional amendment to reform the Electoral College and establish a process for electing the President and Vice President by a national popular vote and should encourage individual States to continue to reform the Electoral College process through such steps as the formation of an interstate compact to award the majority of Electoral College votes to the national popular vote winner.

IN THE HOUSE OF REPRESENTATIVES

SEPTEMBER 14, 2017

Mr. Conyers (for himself, Mr. Nadler, Ms. Lofgren, Mr. Cohen, Mr. Raskin, Mr. Al Green of Texas, Ms.Jackson Lee, Mr. Johnson of Georgia, Mr. Jeffries, Mr. Blumenauer, and Mr. Gutiérrez) submitted the following concurrent resolution; which was referred to the Committee on the Judiciary

CONCURRENT RESOLUTION

Expressing the sense of Congress that Congress and the States should consider a constitutional amendment to reform the Electoral College and establish a process for electing the President and Vice President by a national popular vote and should encourage individual States to continue to reform the Electoral College process through such steps as the formation of an interstate compact to award the majority of Electoral College votes to the national popular vote winner.

Whereas the Supreme Court has held that the "conception of political equality from the Declaration of Independence, to Lincoln's Gettysburg Address, to the 15th, 17th, and 19th Amendments can only mean one thing — one person, one vote;";

Whereas the Electoral College is an anti-democratic method of Presidential selection that has permitted the candidate without a majority of the popular vote to become

President of the United States on five occasions, including the most recent election, in which Hillary Clinton garnered almost 3 million more votes than Electoral College winner Donald Trump;

Whereas the Electoral College lessens the value of votes in the majority of States relative to the value of votes in so-called swing States because a small number of voters in these States can determine the outcome of an election;

Whereas a person could be elected President with potentially less than 22 percent of the popular vote, calling into question his or her political legitimacy;

Whereas the "winner take all" basis of the Electoral College discounts the votes of the millions of people who did not vote for the winning candidate in their States;

Whereas the Electoral College does not act as a check on unqualified candidates as the Framers of the Constitution intended because it is populated by political party loyalists who do not, and often under State law cannot, exercise independent judgment or who do not even meet to deliberate about who should be President, which is why over time there have been very few "faithless" electors, and none that have decided an election's outcome;

Whereas the Electoral College does not protect small-population States and rural areas from domination by large-population States and urban areas and instead encourages candidates to bypass the majority of States, whatever their size, to focus their campaign efforts on a very small number of swing States;

Whereas in the 2016 Presidential election both major party candidates largely bypassed 3 of the 4 largest States by population during the campaign and also skipped campaigning in 12 of the 13 smallest States as well;

Whereas statewide recounts under differing and confusing rules bring neither clarity nor finality to the electoral process, while a national popular vote is far more likely to establish a clear winner, avoiding the necessity of recounts altogether;

Whereas according to Yale Law School Professor Akhil Reed Amar, the Electoral College is an anachronistic institution, its historical development rooted in preserving the political influence of slaveholding States whose enslaved populations were not allowed to vote but three-fifths of whom were counted when determining the number of Electoral College votes allotted to the State;

Whereas proposed amendments to the Constitution reforming the Electoral College have been approved by a two-thirds majority twice in the Senate and once in the House, and more than 700 proposals to eliminate or reform the Electoral College have been introduced; and

Whereas 11 States representing 165 electoral votes have already entered into an interstate compact to cast their electoral votes for the national popular vote winner: Now, therefore, be it

Resolved by the House of Representatives (the Senate concurring), That it is the sense of Congress that—

(1) Congress and the States should consider a constitutional amendment to reform the Electoral College and establish a process for electing the President and Vice President by a national popular vote; and

(2) Congress should encourage the States to continue to reform the Electoral College process through such steps as the formation of an interstate compact to award the majority of Electoral College votes to the national popular vote winner.

1. Do you agree with the reasons given for moving toward a national popular vote?

2. What does "one person, one vote" mean, and how does the Electoral College fit within this concept?

"THE FAITHLESS ELECTOR PROBLEM," BY REPRESENTATIVE BRADLEY BYRNE, FROM THE *CONGRESSIONAL RECORD*, JANUARY 9, 2017

The SPEAKER pro tempore. The Chair recognizes the gentleman from Alabama (Mr. Byrne) for 5 minutes.

Mr. BYRNE. Mr. Speaker, last Friday the House and the Senate met to fulfill our solemn constitutional responsibility to count the votes of electors for President and Vice President. This year the joint session was confronted with a record number of so-called faithless electors-- electors who were supposed to vote for the Presidential candidates named on their States' ballot, but, instead, voted for someone else. Different States handle their faithless electors in different ways. In my view, the joint session rightly fulfilled its constitutional responsibility by simply taking the certified results of each State without intervention. This was in line with precedent set in 1969 and with the text of the Constitution.

Because I believe this decision to be correct, I did not file an objection during the counting process. However, I wish for the Record to contain my views on this matter and to express my concern that an avoidable constitutional crisis on this subject is a very real possibility in the future.

The faithless elector problem has often been seen as academic, but in 2000, Vice President Gore was three faithless electors away from the Presidency. As a point of reference, there were 10 faithless electors in this election. Thus, this is not a matter that should be taken lightly.

Article II, Section 1, Clause 2 of the Constitution gives the States the exclusive power to appoint electors in a manner decided by their State legislatures. Clause 4 provides the sole grant of authority to Congress in the process to determine the time for choosing electors and the day they cast their vote.

The process to count electors is outlined in Clause 3 and identical language which superseded it in the 12th Amendment. It provides that, ``The President of the Senate shall, in the presence of the Senate and the House of Representatives, open all the certificates and the votes shall then be counted. . . .'' Under the 12th Amendment, the persons receiving a majority of the vote ``shall be'' the President and Vice President.

The extent of what Congress' powers are in the counting process has been the subject of over 200 years of debate. The Congressional Record from 1800 includes a lengthy speech by Senator Charles Pinckney, a Framer of the Constitution, who stated that as the Framers wished the President to be independent, ``It never was intended . . . to have given to Congress . . . the right to object to any electoral vote.''

The first successful effort to expand Congress' power in counting did not come until 1865, when Congress adopted a joint House-Senate rule on the subject. Under the rule, no electoral vote that incurred an objection could be counted unless both Houses agreed.

The joint rule was tempered by the Electoral Count Act of 1887, which still governs the counting process to this day. The law allows an objection signed by a House and a Senate Member. However, under the Electoral Count Act, unless there is a case of double returns, no electoral vote regularly given and lawfully certified shall be rejected.

In 1969, Dr. Lloyd Bailey, a Republican elector from North Carolina, was faithless, and the Governor of North Carolina certified the State's electoral certificate with knowledge of his vote.

The House and the Senate thoroughly debated whether Dr. Bailey's vote should be counted, but ultimately voted to reject the challenge. Opponents of the challenge, in my view, properly argued that Congress lacked the power to exclude Dr. Bailey's vote under the Electoral Count Act and, more importantly, Congress had no power to exclude his vote under the Constitution. To do so would be a violation of the rights of the sovereign States.

Some have argued that the Bailey precedent is not applicable when an elector violates his or her State's law in casting a faithless vote. I find this argument constitutionally suspect. Unless no candidate reaches a majority, Congress' role in the counting process appears to be ministerial: to count votes and announce a result.

For that reason, the issue of faithless electors is rightly resolved at the State level, before the results reach Congress. At the present time, however, a hodgepodge of State laws exist to deal with faithless electors, some of which are ill-equipped to handle the problem.

Fortunately, the Uniform Law Commission has proposed the Faithful Presidential Electors Act, which has already been enacted in four States. The

Faithful Presidential Electors Act provides a State-administered pledge of faithfulness, with any attempt by an elector to submit a vote in violation of that pledge constituting a resignation from the office of elector. In such case, the act provides a mechanism for filling an electoral vacancy.

At the conclusion of my remarks, I will include in the Record a copy of the Faithful Presidential Electors Act.

In short, Mr. Speaker, based upon my view of the Constitution, Congress properly handled the issue of faithless electors in this election. This election should, however, serve as a wake-up call to States that further action on their part may be necessary.

UNIFORM FAITHFUL PRESIDENTIAL ELECTORS ACT

(Drafted by the National Conference of Commissioners on Uniform State Laws and by it Approved and Recommended for Enactment in All the States at its Annual Conference Meeting in Its One-Hundred-and-Nineteenth Year in Chicago, Illinois July 9-16, 2010 Without Prefatory Note or Comments)
[Copyright 2010 by National Conference of Commissioners on Uniform State Laws, September 28, 2010]

UNIFORM FAITHFUL PRESIDENTIAL ELECTORS ACT

SECTION 1. SHORT TITLE. This [act] may be cited as the Uniform Faithful Presidential Electors Act.

SECTION 2. DEFINITIONS. In this [act]:

(1) ``Cast'' means accepted by the [Secretary of State] in accordance with Section 7(b).

(2) ``Elector'' means an individual selected as a presidential elector under [applicable state statute] and this [act].

(3) ``President'' means President of the United States.

(4) [``Unaffiliated presidential candidate'' means a candidate for President who qualifies for the general election ballot in this state by means other than nomination by a political party.]

[(5)] ``Vice President'' means Vice President of the United States.

SECTION 3. DESIGNATION OF STATE'S ELECTORS. For each elector position in this state, a political party contesting the position[, or an unaffiliated presidential candidate,] shall submit to the [Secretary of State] the names of two qualified individuals. One of the individuals must be designated ``elector nominee'' and the other ``alternate elector nominee''. Except as otherwise provided in Sections 5 through 8, this state's electors are the winning elector nominees under the laws of this state.

Legislative Note: For a state wishing to accommodate unpledged electors, the following three sentences could be substituted for the first two sentences of Section 3: ``Any political party [or unaffiliated presidential candidate] advancing candidates for elector positions in this state shall submit to the [Secretary of State] the names of two qualified individuals for each elector position to be contested. One of the individuals must be designated ``elector nominee'' and the other ``alternate elector nominee''. Any unpledged candidate for the position of elector who is not nominated by a political party or unaffiliated presidential candidate shall submit to the [Secretary of State], in addition to the individual's own name as ``elector nominee'', the name of another qualified individual designated as ``alternate elector nominee''.''

SECTION 4. PLEDGE. Each elector nominee and alternate elector nominee of a political party shall execute the following pledge: ``If selected for the position of elector, I agree to serve and to mark my ballots for President and Vice President for the nominees for those offices of the party that nominated me.'' [Each elector nominee and alternate elector nominee of an unaffiliated presidential candidate shall execute the following pledge: ``If selected for the position of elector as a nominee of an unaffiliated presidential candidate, I agree to serve and to mark my ballots for that candidate and for that candidate's vice-presidential running mate.''] The executed pledges must accompany the submission of the corresponding names to the [Secretary of State].

Legislative Note: This act does not deal with the possibility of death of a presidential or vice-presidential candidate before the electoral college meetings, or with any other disabling condition or the discovery of disqualifying information. A state may choose to deal separately with one or another of these possibilities.

SECTION 5. CERTIFICATION OF ELECTORS. In submitting this state's certificate of ascertainment as required by 3 U.S.C. Section 6, the [Governor] shall certify this state's electors and state in the certificate that:

(1) the electors will serve as electors unless a vacancy occurs in the office of elector before the end of the meeting at which elector votes are cast, in which case a substitute elector will fill the vacancy; and

(2) if a substitute elector is appointed to fill a vacancy, the [Governor] will submit an amended certificate of ascertainment stating the names on the final list of this state's electors.

SECTION 6. PRESIDING OFFICER; ELECTOR VACANCY.

(a) The [Secretary of State] shall preside at the meeting of electors described in Section 7.

(b) The position of an elector not present to vote is vacant. The [Secretary of State] shall appoint an individual as a substitute elector to fill a vacancy as follows:

(1) if the alternate elector is present to vote, by appointing the alternate elector for the vacant position;

(2) if the alternate elector for the vacant position is not present to vote, by appointing an elector chosen by lot from among the alternate electors present to vote who were nominated by the same political party [or unaffiliated presidential candidate];

(3) if the number of alternate electors present to vote is insufficient to fill any vacant position pursuant to paragraphs (1) and (2), by appointing any immediately available individual who is qualified to serve as an elector and chosen through nomination by and plurality vote of the remaining electors, including nomination and vote by a single elector if only one remains;

(4) if there is a tie between at least two nominees for substitute elector in a vote conducted under paragraph (3), by appointing an elector chosen by lot from among those nominees; or

(5) if all elector positions are vacant and cannot be filled pursuant to paragraphs (1) through (4), by appointing a single presidential elector, with remaining vacant positions to be filled under paragraph (3) and, if necessary, paragraph (4).

(c) To qualify as a substitute elector under subsection (b), an individual who has not executed the pledge required under Section 4 shall execute the following pledge: ``I agree to serve and to mark my ballots for President and Vice President consistent with the pledge of the individual to whose elector position I have succeeded.''.

Legislative Note: As with Sections 3 and 4, adjustment of this Section is required for any state where unpledged electors are permissible. For a state wishing to accommodate unpledged electors, the language of subsections (b)(2), (b)(3), and (c) could be changed to the following:

(b)(2): ``if the alternate elector for the vacant position is not present to vote but other alternate electors who were nominated by the same political party [or unaffiliated presidential candidate] are present, by appointing an elector chosen by lot from among those alternate electors of the same political party [or of the same unaffiliated presidential candidate] .''

(b)(3): ``if the vacant position is that of an unpledged elector and the alternate elector for that vacant position is not present to vote, or if there otherwise are no alternate electors eligible for the vacant position under paragraphs (1) and (2), by appointing any immediately available individual who is qualified to serve as an elector and has been chosen through nomination by and plurality vote of the remaining electors, including nomination and vote by a single elector if only one remains.''

(c): ``To qualify as a substitute elector for a vacant position associated with an elector who had executed a pledge, an individual who has not executed the pledge required under Section 4 shall execute the following pledge: ``I agree to serve and to mark my ballots for President and Vice President consistent with the pledge of the individual to whose elector position I have succeeded''.''

SECTION 7. ELECTOR VOTING.

(a) At the time designated for elector voting and after all vacant positions have been filled under Section 6, the [Secretary of State] shall provide each elector with a presidential and a vice-presidential ballot. The elector shall mark the elector's presidential and vice-presidential ballots with the elector's votes for the offices of President and Vice President, respectively, along with the elector's signature and the elector's legibly printed name.

(b) Except as otherwise provided by law of this state other than this [act], each elector shall present both completed ballots to the [Secretary of State], who shall examine the ballots and accept as cast all ballots of electors whose votes are consistent with their pledges executed under Section 4 or 6(c). Except as otherwise provided by law of this state other than this [act], the [Secretary of State] may not accept and may not count either an elector's presidential or vice-presidential ballot if the elector has not marked both ballots or has marked a ballot in violation of the elector's pledge.

(c) An elector who refuses to present a ballot, presents an unmarked ballot, or presents a ballot marked in violation of the elector's pledge executed under Section 4 or 6(c) vacates the office of elector, creating a vacant position to be filled under Section 6.

(d) The [Secretary of State] shall distribute ballots to and collect ballots from a substitute elector and repeat the process under this section of examining ballots, declaring and filling vacant positions as required, and recording appropriately completed ballots from the substituted electors, until all of this state's electoral votes have been cast and recorded.

SECTION 8. ELECTOR REPLACEMENT; ASSOCIATED CERTIFICATES.

(a) After the vote of this state's electors is completed, if the final list of electors differs from any list that the [Governor] previously included on a certificate of ascertainment prepared and transmitted under 3 U.S.C. Section

6, the [Secretary of State] immediately shall prepare an amended certificate of ascertainment and transmit it to the [Governor] for the [Governor's] signature.

(b) The [Governor] immediately shall deliver the signed amended certificate of ascertainment to the [Secretary of State] and a signed duplicate original of the amended certificate of ascertainment to all individuals entitled to receive this state's certificate of ascertainment, indicating that the amended certificate of ascertainment is to be substituted for the certificate of ascertainment previously submitted.

(c) The [Secretary of State] shall prepare a certificate of vote. The electors on the final list shall sign the certificate. The [Secretary of State] shall process and transmit the signed certificate with the amended certificate of ascertainment under 3 U.S.C. Sections 9, 10, and 11.

SECTION 9. UNIFORMITY OF APPLICATION AND CONSTRUCTION. In applying and construing this uniform act, consideration must be given to the need to promote uniformity of the law with respect to its subject matter among states that enact it.

SECTION 10. REPEALS. The following are repealed:

(1) . . .

(2) . . .

(3). . .

SECTION 11. EFFECTIVE DATE. This [act] takes effect. . :

1. What is a faithless elector?

2. Does the speaker agree with or disagree with the legality of faithless electors? Why or why not?

"THE ELECTORAL COLLEGE," BY SENATOR HARRY REID, FROM THE *CONGRESSIONAL RECORD*, NOVEMBER 16, 2016

Mr. REID. Mr. President, election day was tough for a lot of Americans. To say things didn't go the way we wanted on this side of the aisle would be a gross understatement. America is still reeling from this, and there will be even more concern in a few days when the final vote tally comes because Hillary Clinton will have gotten more than 2 million votes more than Donald Trump.

So I think it speaks volumes that a Democratic Senator entered legislation yesterday that will take a look at the electoral college system. This should not be a partisan issue. It should be an issue that committees of jurisdiction in this body take a look at. Let's listen to some experts talk about it and find out if the system is working very well. It was set up a long time ago, and maybe it should be changed. So, I think it is something we need to take a look at.

It is interesting that just in the last few years--in this century--we have had two winners of elections that got less votes than the losers. I am sorry. We have two elections this century where the losers got more votes than the winners. So we need to take a look at that, and so I hope something is done on a bipartisan basis because no one knows what is going to happen 4 years from now, 8 years from now, 12 years from now. It is something that should be looked at. It is very important for us as a country to take another look at the electoral college system.

1. Why does Senator Reid feel it is important to reconsider the Electoral College?

CHAPTER 3

WHAT THE COURTS SAY

The courts, including the Supreme Court, have heard numerous cases related to the Electoral College, with some dating back to the late nineteenth century. These cases give us a good sense of what controversies surrounding the Electoral College have been the most pressing for citizens and activists and provide a grounding in the constitutional scholarship around the Electoral College. As one of the most important precedent-setting bodies in the country, the Supreme Court has handed down crucial interpretations of the Electoral College and its place in our election system that will influence the extent to which reforms can be implemented by the state or federal government.

MCPHERSON V. BLACKER, FROM THE SUPREME COURT, OCTOBER 17, 1892

The validity of a state law providing for the appointment of electors of President and Vice President having been drawn in question before the highest tribunal of a state as repugnant to the laws and Constitution of the United States, and that court having decided in favor of its validity, this Court has jurisdiction to review the judgment under Rev.Stat. § 709.

Under the second clause of Article II of the Constitution, the legislatures of the several states have exclusive power to direct the manner in which the electors of President and Vice President shall be appointed.

Such appointment may be made by the legislatures directly, or by popular vote in districts, or by general ticket, as may be provided by the legislature.

If the terms of the clause left the question of power in doubt, contemporaneous and continuous subsequent practical construction has determined the question as above stated.

The second clause of Article II of the Constitution was not amended by the Fourteenth and Fifteenth Amendments, and they do not limit the power of appointment to the particular manner pursued at the time of the adoption of these amendments or secure to every male inhabitant of a state, being a citizen of the United States, the right from the time of his majority to vote for presidential electors.

A state law fixing a date for the meeting of electors differing from that prescribed by the act of Congress is not thereby wholly invalidated, but the date may be rejected and the law stand.

William McPherson, Jr., Jay A. Hubbell, J. Henry Carstens, Charles E. Hiscock, Otto Ihling, Philip T. Colgrove, Conrad G. Swensburg, Henry A. Haigh, James H. White, Fred. Slocum, Justus S. Stearns, John Millen, Julius T. Hannah, and J. H. Comstock filed their petition and affidavits in the Supreme Court of the State of Michigan on May 2, 1892, as nominees for presidential electors, against Robert R. Blacker, Secretary of State of Michigan, praying that the court declare the Act of the legislature approved May 1, 1891, Act No. 50, Public Acts of Michigan of 1891, entitled "An act to provide for the election of electors of President and Vice-President of the United States, and to repeal all other acts and parts of acts in conflict herewith," void and of no effect, and that a writ of mandamus be directed to be issued to the said Secretary of State commanding him to cause to be delivered to the sheriff of each county in the state, between the first of July and the first of September, 1892, "a notice in writing that at the next general election in this state, to be held on Tuesday, the 8th day of November, 1892, there will be chosen (among other officers to be named in said notice) as many electors of President and Vice-President of the United States as this state may be entitled to elect senators and representatives in the Congress."

The statute of Michigan (Howell's Ann.Stats. of Michigan, 133, c. 9) provided: "The secretary of the state shall, between the first day of July and the first day of September preceding a general election, direct and cause to be delivered to the sheriff of each county in this state a notice in writing that at the next general election, there will be chosen as many of the following officers as are to be elected at such general election, viz.: a governor, lieutenant governor, secretary of state, state treasurer, auditor general, attorney general, superintendent of public instruction, commissioner of state land office, members of the state board of education, electors of President and Vice-President of the United States, and a representative in Congress for the district to which each of such counties shall belong."

A rule to show cause having been issued, the respondent, as Secretary of State, answered the petition, and denied that he had refused to give the notice thus required, but he said "that it has always been the custom in the office of the secretary of state, in giving notices under said section 147, to state in the notice the number of electors that should be printed on the ticket in each voting precinct in each county in this state, and following such custom with reference to such notice, it is the intention of this respondent in giving notice under section 147 to state in said notice that there will be elected one presidential elector at large and one district presidential elector and two alternate presidential electors, one for the elector at large and one for the district presidential elector, in each voting precinct, so that the election may be held under and in accordance with the provisions of Act No. 50 of the Public Acts of the State of Michigan of 1891."

By an amended answer, the respondent claimed the same benefit as if he had demurred.

Relators relied in their petition upon various grounds as invalidating Act No. 50 of the Public Acts of Michigan of 1891, and, among them, that the act was void because in conflict with clause two of section one of Article II of the Constitution of the United States, and with the Fourteenth Amendment to that instrument, and also in some of its provisions in conflict with the Act of Congress of February

3, 1887, entitled "An act to fix the day for the meeting of the electors of President and Vice-President and to provide for and regulate the counting of the votes for President and Vice-President, and the decision of questions arising thereon." The Supreme Court of Michigan unanimously held that none of the objections urged against the validity of the act were tenable; that it did not conflict with clause two of section one of Article II of the Constitution, or with the Fourteenth Amendment thereof, and that the law was only inoperative so far as in conflict with the law of Congress in a matter in reference to which Congress had the right to legislate. The opinion of the court will be found reported, in advance of the official series, in 52 N.W. 469.

Judgment was given, June 17, 1892, denying the writ of mandamus, whereupon a writ of error was allowed to this Court.

The October term, 1892, commenced on Monday, October 10, and on Tuesday, October 11, the first day upon which the application could be made, a motion to advance the case was submitted by counsel, granted at once in view of the exigency disclosed upon the face of the papers, and the cause heard that day. The attention of the court having been called to other provisions of the election laws of Michigan than those supposed to be immediately involved (Act No. 190, Public Acts of Michigan 1891, pp. 258, 263), the Chief Justice, on Monday, October 17, announced the conclusions of the court and directed the entry of judgment affirming the judgment of the Supreme Court of Michigan, and ordering the mandate to issue at once, it being stated that this was done because immediate action under the state statutes was apparently required and might be affected by delay, but it was added that the court would thereafter file an opinion stating fully the grounds of the decision.

Act No. 50 of the Public Acts of 1891 of Michigan is as follows:

"An act to provide for the election of electors of President and Vice-President of the United States, and to repeal all other acts and parts of acts in conflict herewith."

"SECTION 1. *The people of the State of Michigan enact,* That at the general election next preceding the choice of President and Vice-President of the United States, there shall be elected as many electors of President and Vice-President as this state may be entitled to elect of senators and representatives in Congress in the following manner, that is to say, there shall be elected by the electors of the districts hereinafter defined one elector of President and Vice-President of the United States in each district, who shall be known and designated on the ballot, respectively, as 'eastern district elector of President and Vice-President of the United States at large,' and 'western district elector of President and Vice-President of the United States at large.' There shall also be elected, in like manner, two alternate electors of President and Vice-President, who shall be known and designated on the ballot as 'eastern district alternate elector of President and Vice-President of the United States at large' and 'western district alternate elector of President and Vice-President of the United States at large,' for which purpose the first, second, sixth, seventh, eighth, and tenth congressional districts shall compose one district, to be known as the 'Eastern Electoral District,' and the third, fourth, fifth, ninth, eleventh, and twelfth congressional districts shall compose the other district, to be known as the 'Western Electoral District.' There shall also be elected, by the electors in each congressional district into which the state is or shall be divided, one electors of President and Vice-President, and one alternate elector of President and Vice-President, the ballots for which shall designate the number of the congressional district and the persons to be voted for therein, as 'district elector' and 'alternate district elector' of President and Vice-President of the United States, respectively."

"SEC. 2. The counting, canvassing, and certifying of the votes cast for said electors at large and their alternates, and said district electors and their alternates, shall be done as near as may be in the same manner as is now provided by law for the election of electors or President and Vice-President of the United States."

"SEC. 3. The Secretary of State shall prepare three lists of the names of the electors and the alternate electors, procure thereto the signature of the governor, affix the seal of the state to the same, and deliver such certificates thus signed and sealed to one of the electors, on or before the first Wednesday of December next following said general election. In case of death, disability, refusal to act, or neglect to attend, by the hour of twelve o'clock at noon of said day, of either of said electors at large, the duties of the office shall be performed by the alternate electors at large, that is to say: the eastern district alternate elector at large shall supply the place of the eastern district elector at large, and the western district alternate elector at large shall supply the place of the western district elector at large. In like case, the alternate congressional district elector shall supply the place of the congressional district elector. In case two or more persons have an equal and the highest number of votes for any office created by this act as canvassed by the board of state canvassers, the legislature in joint convention shall choose one of said persons to fill such office, and it shall be the duty of the governor to convene the legislature in special session for such purpose immediately upon such determination by said board of state canvassers."

"SEC. 4. The said electors of President and Vice-President shall convene in the Senate chamber at the capital of the state at the hour of twelve o'clock at noon, on the first Wednesday of December immediately following their election, and shall proceed to perform the duties of such electors as required by the Constitution and the laws of the United States. The alternate electors shall also be in attendance, but shall take no part in the proceedings, except as herein provided."

"SEC. 5. Each of said electors and alternate electors shall receive the sum of five dollars for each day's attendance at the meetings of the electors as above provided, and five cents per mile for the actual and necessary distance traveled each way in going to and returning from said place of meeting, the same to be paid by the state treasurer upon the allowance of the board of state auditors."

"SEC. 6. All acts and parts of acts in conflict with the provisions of this act are hereby repealed." Approved May 1, 1891.

Section 211 of Howell's Annotated Statutes of Michigan (volume 1, c. 9, p. 145) reads:

"For the purpose of canvassing and ascertaining the votes given for electors of President and Vice-President of the United States, the board of state canvassers shall meet on the Wednesday next after the third Monday of November, or on such other day before that time as the Secretary of State shall appoint, and the powers, duties, and proceedings of said board, and of the Secretary of State, in sending for, examining, ascertaining, determining, certifying, and recording the votes and results of the election of such electors, shall be in all respects, as near as may be, as hereinbefore provided in relation to sending for, examining, ascertaining, determining, certifying, and recording the votes and results of the election of state officers."

Section 240 of Howell's Statutes, in force prior to May 1, 1891, provided:

"At the general election next preceding the choice of President and Vice-President of the United States, there shall be elected by general ticket as many electors of President and Vice-President as this state may be entitled to elect of senators and representatives in Congress."

The following are sections of Article VIII of the Constitution of Michigan:

"SEC. 4. The secretary of state, state treasurer, and commissioner of the state land office shall constitute a board of state auditors, to examine and adjust all claims against the state, not otherwise provided for by general law. They shall constitute a board of state canvassers, to determine the result of all elections for governor, lieutenant governor, and state officers, and of such other officers as shall by law be referred to them."

"SEC. 5. In case two or more persons have an equal and the highest number of votes for any office, as canvassed by the board of state canvassers, the legislature in joint convention shall choose one of said persons to fill such office. When the determination of the board of state canvassers is contested, the legislature in joint convention shall decide which person is elected." (1 Howell's Ann.Stats.Mich. 57.)

Reference was also made in argument to the act of Congress of February 3, 1887, to fix the day for the meeting of the electors of President and Vice-President, and to provide for and regulate and counting of the votes. 24 Stat. 373, c. 90.

1. According to this case, how are electors selected?

2. What was the basis for this case? Why did the plaintiff feel it was unconstitutional and did the court agree?

EXCERPT FROM *RAY, CHAIRMAN OF THE STATE DEMOCRATIC EXECUTIVE COMMITTEE OF ALABAMA V. BLAIR*, FROM THE US SUPREME COURT, APRIL 15, 1952

Where a state authorizes a political party to choose its nominees for Presidential Electors in a state-controlled party primary election and to fix the qualifications for the candidates, it is not violative of the Federal Constitution for the party to require the candidates for the office of Presidential Elector to take a pledge to support the nominees of the party's National Convention for President and Vice-President or for the party's officers to refuse to certify as a candidate for Presidential Elector a person otherwise qualified who refuses to take such a pledge. Pp. 343 U. S. 215-231.

1. Presidential Electors exercise a federal function in balloting for President and Vice-President, but they are not federal officers. They act by authority of the state, which, in turn, receives its authority from the Federal Constitution. Pp. 343 U. S. 224-225.

2. Exclusion of a candidate in a party primary by a state or political party because such candidate will not pledge to support the party's nominees is a method of securing party candidates in the general election who are pledged to the philosophy and leadership of that party, and it is an exercise of the state's right under Art. II, § 1, to appoint electors in such manner as it may choose. *United States v. Classic,* 313 U. S. 299, and *Smith v. Allwright,* 321 U. S. 649, distinguished. Pp. 343 U. S. 225-227.

3. The Twelfth Amendment does not bar a political party from requiring of a candidate for Presidential Elector in its primary a pledge to support the nominees of its National Convention. Pp. 343 U. S. 228-231.

4. The requirement of such a pledge does not deny equal protection or due process under the Fourteenth Amendment. *Nixon v. Herndon,* 273 U. S. 536, distinguished. P. 226, n 14.

257 Ala. ___, 57 So.2d 395, reversed.

The Alabama Supreme Court upheld, on federal constitutional grounds, a peremptory writ of mandamus requiring petitioner, the Chairman of the State Executive Committee of the Democratic Party, to certify respondent as a candidate for Presidential Elector in a Democratic Primary which was to be held on May 6, 1952. 257 Ala. ___, 57 So.2d 395. This Court granted certiorari. 343 U.S. 901. In a per curiam decision announced on April 3, 1952, in advance of the preparation of this opinion, this Court reversed that judgment. 343 U. S. 154. This opinion states the reasons for that decision.

1. According to this case, what requirements are placed on political parties as they choose electors?

EXCERPT FROM *BUSH ET AL. V. GORE ET AL.*, FROM THE US SUPREME COURT, DECEMBER 12, 2000

On December 8, 2000, the Supreme Court of Florida ordered that the Circuit Court of Leon County tabulate by hand 9,000 ballots in Miami-Dade County. It also ordered the inclusion in the certified vote totals of 215 votes identified in Palm Beach County and 168 votes identified in Miami-Dade County for Vice President Albert Gore, Jr., and Senator Joseph Lieberman, Democratic candidates for President and Vice President. The State Supreme Court noted that petitioner George W. Bush asserted that the net gain for Vice President Gore in Palm Beach County was 176 votes, and directed the Circuit Court to resolve that dispute on remand. *Gore v. Harris,* 772 So. 2d 1243, 1248, n. 6. The court further held that relief would require manual recounts in all Florida counties where so-called "undervotes" had not been subject to manual tabulation. The court ordered all manual recounts to begin at once. Governor Bush and Richard Cheney, Republican candidates for President and Vice President, filed an emergency application for a stay of this mandate. On December 9, we granted the application, treated the application as a petition for a writ of certiorari, and granted certiorari. *Post,* p. 1046.

The proceedings leading to the present controversy are discussed in some detail in our opinion in *Bush v. Palm Beach County Canvassing Bd., ante,* p. 70 *(per curiam) (Bush I).* On November 8, 2000, the day following the Presidential election, the Florida Division of Elections reported that petitioner Bush had received 2,909,135 votes, and respondent Gore had received 2,907,351 votes, a margin of 1,784 for Governor Bush. Because Governor Bush's margin of victory was less than "one-half of a percent ... of the votes cast," an automatic machine recount was conducted under § 102.141(4) of the Florida Election Code, the results of which showed Governor Bush still winning the race but by a diminished margin. Vice President Gore then sought manual recounts in Volusia, Palm Beach, Broward, and Miami-Dade Counties, pursuant to Florida's election protest provisions. Fla. Stat. Ann. § 102.166 (Supp. 2001). A dispute arose concerning the deadline for local county canvassing boards to submit their returns to the Secretary of State (Secretary). The Secretary declined to waive the November 14 deadline imposed by statute. §§ 102.111, 102.112. The Florida Supreme Court, however, set the deadline at November 26. We granted certiorari and vacated the Florida Supreme Court's decision, finding considerable uncertainty as to the grounds on which it was based. *Bush I, ante,* at 78. On December 11, the Florida Supreme Court issued a decision on remand reinstating that date. *Palm Beach County Canvassing Bd. v. Harris,* 772 So. 2d 1273, 1290.

On November 26, the Florida Elections Canvassing Commission certified the results of the election and declared Governor Bush the winner of Florida's 25 electoral votes. On November 27, Vice President Gore, pursuant to Florida's contest provisions, filed a complaint in Leon County Circuit Court contesting the certification. Fla. Stat. Ann. § 102.168 (Supp. 2001). He sought relief pursuant to § 102.168(3)(c), which provides that "[r]eceipt of a number of illegal votes or rejection of a number of legal votes sufficient to change or place in doubt the result of the election" shall be grounds for a contest. The Circuit Court denied relief, stating that Vice President Gore failed to meet his burden of proof. He appealed to the First District Court of Appeal, which certified the matter to the Florida Supreme Court.

Accepting jurisdiction, the Florida Supreme Court affirmed in part and reversed in part. *Gore v. Harris,* 772 So. 2d 1243 (2000). The court held that the Circuit Court had been correct to reject Vice President Gore's challenge to the results certified in Nassau County and his challenge to the Palm Beach County Canvassing Board's determination that 3,300 ballots cast in that county were not, in the statutory phrase, "legal votes."

The Supreme Court held that Vice President Gore had satisfied his burden of proof under § 102.168(3)(c) with respect to his challenge to Miami-Dade County's failure to tabulate, by manual count, 9,000 ballots on which the machines had failed to detect a vote for President ("undervotes"). *Id.,* at 1256. Noting the closeness of the election, the court explained that "[o]n this record, there can be no question that there are legal votes within the 9,000 uncounted votes sufficient to place the results of this election in doubt." *Id.,* at 1261.

A "legal vote," as determined by the Supreme Court, is "one in which there is a 'clear indication of the intent of the voter.'" *Id.,* at 1257. The court therefore ordered a hand recount of the 9,000 ballots in Miami-Dade County. Observing that the contest provisions vest broad discretion in the circuit judge to "provide any relief appropriate under such circumstances," § 102.168(8), the Supreme Court further held that the Circuit Court could order "the Supervisor of Elections and the Canvassing Boards, as well as the necessary public officials, in all counties that have not conducted a manual recount or tabulation of the undervotes ... to do so forthwith, said tabulation to take place in the individual counties where the ballots are located." *Id.,* at 1262.

The Supreme Court also determined that Palm Beach County and Miami-Dade County, in their earlier manual recounts, had identified a net gain of 215 and 168 legal votes, respectively, for Vice President Gore. *Id.,* at 1260. Rejecting the Circuit Court's conclusion that Palm Beach County lacked the authority to include the 215 net votes submitted past the November 26 deadline, the Supreme Court explained that the deadline was not intended to exclude votes identified after that date through ongoing manual recounts. As to Miami-Dade County, the court concluded that although the 168 votes identified were the result of a partial recount, they were "legal votes [that] could change the outcome of the election." *Ibid.* The Supreme Court therefore directed the Circuit Court to include those totals in the certified results, subject to resolution of the actual vote total from the Miami-Dade partial recount.

The petition presents the following questions: whether the Florida Supreme Court established new standards for resolving Presidential election contests, thereby violating Art. II, § 1, cl. 2, of the United States Constitution and failing to comply with 3 U. S. C. § 5, and whether the use of standardless manual recounts violates the Equal Protection and Due Process Clauses. With respect to the equal protection question, we find a violation of the Equal Protection Clause.

II

A

The closeness of this election, and the multitude of legal challenges which have followed in its wake, have brought into sharp focus a common, if heretofore unnoticed, phenomenon. Nationwide statistics reveal that an estimated 2% of ballots cast do not register a vote for President for whatever reason, including deliberately choosing no candidate at all or some voter error, such as voting for two candidates or insufficiently marking a ballot. See Ho, More Than 2M Ballots Uncounted, AP Online (Nov. 28, 2000); Kelley, Balloting Problems Not Rare But Only in a Very Close Election Do Mistakes and Mismarking Make a Difference, Omaha World-Herald (Nov. 15,2000). In certifying election results, the votes eligible for inclusion in the certification are the votes meeting the properly established legal requirements.

This case has shown that punchcard balloting machines can produce an unfortunate number of ballots which are not punched in a clean, complete way by the voter. After the current counting, it is likely legislative bodies nationwide will examine ways to improve the mechanisms and machinery for voting.

B

The individual citizen has no federal constitutional right to vote for electors for the President of the United States unless and until the state legislature chooses a statewide election as the means to implement its power to appoint members of the electoral college. U. S. Const., Art. II, § 1. This is the source for the statement in *McPherson v. Blacker,* 146 U. S. 1, 35 (1892), that the state legislature's power to select the manner for appointing electors is plenary; it may, if it so chooses, select the electors itself, which indeed was the manner used by state legislatures in several States for many years after the framing of our Constitution. *Id.,* at 28-33. History has now favored the voter, and in each of the several States the citizens themselves vote for Presidential electors. When the state legislature vests the right to vote for President in its people, the right to vote as the legislature has prescribed is fundamental; and one source of its fundamental nature lies in the equal weight accorded to each vote and the equal dignity owed to each voter. The State, of course, after granting the franchise in the special context of Article II, can take back the power to appoint electors. See id., at 35 (" '[T]here is no doubt of the right of the legislature to resume the power at any time, for it can neither be taken away nor abdicated'") (quoting

The right to vote is protected in more than the initial allocation of the franchise. Equal protection applies as well to the manner of its exercise. Having once granted the right to vote on equal terms, the State may not, by later arbitrary and disparate treatment, value one person's vote over that of another. See, *e. g., Harper v. Virginia Bd. of*

WHAT THE COURTS SAY

Elections, 383 U. S. 663, 665 (1966) ("[O]nce the franchise is granted to the electorate, lines may not be drawn which are inconsistent with the Equal Protection Clause of the Fourteenth Amendment"). It must be remembered that "the right of suffrage can be denied by a debasement or dilution of the weight of a citizen's vote just as effectively as by wholly prohibiting the free exercise of the franchise." *Reynolds v. Sims,* 377 U. S. 533, 555 (1964).

There is no difference between the two sides of the present controversy on these basic propositions. Respondents say that the very purpose of vindicating the right to vote justifies the recount procedures now at issue. The question before us, however, is whether the recount procedures the Florida Supreme Court has adopted are consistent with its obligation to avoid arbitrary and disparate treatment of the members of its electorate.

Much of the controversy seems to revolve around ballot cards designed to be perforated by a stylus but which, either through error or deliberate omission, have not been perforated with sufficient precision for a machine to register the perforations. In some cases a piece of the card-a chad-is hanging, say, by two corners. In other cases there is no separation at all, just an indentation.

The Florida Supreme Court has ordered that the intent of the voter be discerned from such ballots. For purposes of resolving the equal protection challenge, it is not necessary to decide whether the Florida Supreme Court had the authority under the legislative scheme for resolving election disputes to define what a legal vote is and to mandate a manual recount implementing that definition. The recount mechanisms implemented in response to the decisions of the Florida Supreme Court do not satisfy the minimum requirement for nonarbitrary treatment of voters necessary to secure the fundamental right. Florida's basic command for the count of legally cast votes is to consider the "intent of the voter." 772 So. 2d, at 1262. This is unobjectionable as an abstract proposition and a starting principle. The problem inheres in the absence of specific standards to ensure its equal application. The formulation of uniform rules to determine intent based on these recurring circum-stances is practicable and, we conclude, necessary.

The law does not refrain from searching for the intent of the actor in a multitude of circumstances; and in some cases the general command to ascertain intent is not susceptible to much further refinement. In this instance, however, the question is not whether to believe a witness but how to interpret the marks or holes or scratches on an inanimate object, a piece of cardboard or paper which, it is said, might not have registered as a vote during the machine count. The factfinder confronts a thing, not a person. The search for intent can be confined by specific rules designed to ensure uniform treatment.

The want of those rules here has led to unequal eval-uation of ballots in various respects. See id., at 1267 (Wells, C. J., dissenting) ("Should a county canvassing board count or not count a 'dimpled chad' where the voter is able to successfully dislodge the chad in every other contest on that ballot? Here, the county canvassing boards disagree"). As seems to have been acknowledged at oral argument, the standards for accepting or rejecting contested ballots might vary not only from county to county but indeed within a single county from one recount team to another.

The record provides some examples. A monitor in Miami-Dade County testified at trial that he observed that three members of the county canvassing board applied different standards in defining a legal vote. 3 Tr. 497, 499 (Dec. 3, 2000). And testimony at trial also revealed that at least one county changed its evaluative standards during the counting process. Palm Beach County, for example, began the process with a 1990 guideline which precluded counting completely attached chads, switched to a rule that considered a vote to be legal if any light could be seen through a chad, changed back to the 1990 rule, and then abandoned any pretense of a *per se* rule, only to have a court order that the county consider dimpled chads legal. This is not a process with sufficient guarantees of equal treatment.

An early case in our one-person, one-vote jurisprudence arose when a State accorded arbitrary and disparate treatment to voters in its different counties. *Gray v. Sanders,* 372 U. S. 368 (1963). The Court found a constitutional violation. We relied on these principles in the context of the Presidential selection process in *Moore v. Ogilvie,* 394 U. S. 814 (1969), where we invalidated a county-based procedure that diluted the influence of citizens in larger counties in the nominating process. There we observed that "[t]he idea that one group can be granted greater voting strength than another is hostile to the one man, one vote basis of our representative government." *Id.,* at 819.

The State Supreme Court ratified this uneven treatment. It mandated that the recount totals from two counties, Miami-Dade and Palm Beach, be included in the certified total. The court also appeared to hold *sub silentio* that the recount totals from Broward County, which were not completed until after the original November 14 certification by the Secretary, were to be considered part of the new certified vote totals even though the county certification was not contested by Vice President Gore. Yet each of the counties used varying standards to determine what was a legal vote. Broward County used a more forgiving standard than Palm Beach County, and uncovered almost three times as many new votes, a result markedly disproportionate to the difference in population between the counties.

In addition, the recounts in these three counties were not limited to so-called undervotes but extended to all of the ballots. The distinction has real consequences. A manual recount of all ballots identifies not only those ballots which show no vote but also those which contain more than one, the so-called overvotes. Neither category will be counted by the machine. This is not a trivial concern. At oral argument, respondents estimated there are as many as 110,000 overvotes statewide. As a result, the citizen whose ballot was not read by a machine because he failed to vote for a candidate in a way readable by a machine may still have his vote counted in a manual recount; on the other hand, the citizen who marks two candidates in a way discernible by the machine will not have the same opportunity to have his vote count, even if a manual examination of the ballot would reveal the requisite indicia of intent. Furthermore, the citizen who marks two candidates, only one of which is discernible by the machine, will have his vote counted even though it should have been read as an invalid ballot. The State Supreme Court's inclusion of vote counts based on these variant standards exemplifies concerns with the remedial processes that were under way.

That brings the analysis to yet a further equal protection problem. The votes certified by the court included a partial total from one county, Miami-Dade. The Florida Supreme Court's decision thus gives no assurance that the recounts included in a final certification must be complete. Indeed, it is respondents' submission that it would be consistent with the rules of the recount procedures to include whatever partial counts are done by the time of final certification, and we interpret the Florida Supreme Court's decision to permit this. See 772 So. 2d, at 1261-1262, n. 21 (noting "practical difficulties" may control outcome of election, but certifying partial Miami-Dade total nonetheless). This accommodation no doubt results from the truncated contest period established by the Florida Supreme Court in *Palm Beach County Canvassing Bd. v. Harris*, at respondents' own urging. The press of time does not diminish the constitutional concern. A desire for speed is not a general excuse for ignoring equal protection guarantees.

In addition to these difficulties the actual process by which the votes were to be counted under the Florida Supreme Court's decision raises further concerns. That order did not specify who would recount the ballots. The county canvassing boards were forced to pull together ad hoc teams of judges from various Circuits who had no previous training in handling and interpreting ballots. Furthermore, while others were permitted to observe, they were prohibited from objecting during the recount.

The recount process, in its features here described, is inconsistent with the minimum procedures necessary to protect the fundamental right of each voter in the special instance of a statewide recount under the authority of a single state judicial officer. Our consideration is limited to the present circumstances, for the problem of equal protection in election processes generally presents many complexities.

The question before the Court is not whether local entities, in the exercise of their expertise, may develop different systems for implementing elections. Instead, we are presented with a situation where a state court with the power to assure uniformity has ordered a statewide recount with minimal procedural safeguards. When a court orders a statewide remedy, there must be at least some assurance that the rudimentary requirements of equal treatment and fundamental fairness are satisfied.

Given the Court's assessment that the recount process underway was probably being conducted in an unconstitutional manner, the Court stayed the order directing the recount so it could hear this case and render an expedited decision. The contest provision, as it was mandated by the State Supreme Court, is not well calculated to sustain the confidence that all citizens must have in the outcome of elections. The State has not shown that its procedures include the necessary safeguards. The problem, for instance, of the estimated 110,000 overvotes has not been addressed, although Chief Justice Wells called attention to the concern in his dissenting opinion. See 772 So. 2d, at 1264, n. 26.

Upon due consideration of the difficulties identified to this point, it is obvious that the recount cannot be conducted in compliance with the requirements of equal protection and due process without substantial additional work. It would require not only the adoption (after opportunity for argument) of adequate statewide standards for determining what is a legal vote, and practicable procedures to implement them, but also orderly judicial review of any disputed matters that might arise. In addition, the Secretary has advised that the recount of only a portion of the ballots requires that the vote tabulation equipment be used to screen out undervotes, a function for which the machines were not designed. If a recount of overvotes were also required, perhaps even a second screening would be necessary. Use of the equipment for this purpose, and any new software developed for it, would have to be evaluated for accuracy by the Secretary, as required by Fla. Stat. Ann. § 101.015 (Supp. 2001).

The Supreme Court of Florida has said that the legislature intended the State's electors to "participat[e] fully in the federal electoral process," as provided in 3 U. S. C. § 5. 772 So. 2d, at 1289; see also *Palm Beach County Canvassing Bd. v. Harris,* 772 So. 2d 1220, 1237 (Fla. 2000). That statute, in turn, requires that any controversy or contest that is designed to lead to a conclusive selection of electors be completed by December 12. That date is upon us, and there is no recount procedure in place under the State Supreme Court's order that comports with minimal constitutional standards. Because it is evident that any recount seeking to meet the December 12 date will be unconstitutional for the reasons we have discussed, we reverse the judgment of the Supreme Court of Florida ordering a recount to proceed.

Seven Justices of the Court agree that there are constitutional problems with the recount ordered by the Florida Supreme Court that demand a remedy. See *post,* at 134 (SOUTER, J., dissenting); *post,* at 145-146 (BREYER, J., dissenting). The only disagreement is as to the remedy. Because the Florida Supreme Court has said that the Florida Legislature intended to obtain the safe-harbor benefits of 3 U. S. C. § 5, JUSTICE BREYER'S proposed remedy-remanding to the Florida Supreme Court for its ordering of a constitutionally proper contest until December 18-contemplates action in violation of the Florida Election Code, and hence could not be part of an "appropriate" order authorized by Fla. Stat. Ann. § 102.168(8) (Supp. 2001).

***

None are more conscious of the vital limits on judicial authority than are the Members of this Court, and none stand more in admiration of the Constitution's design to leave the selection of the President to the people, through their legislatures, and to the political sphere. When contending parties invoke the process of the courts, however, it becomes our unsought responsibility to resolve the federal and constitutional issues the judicial system has been forced to confront.

The judgment of the Supreme Court of Florida is reversed, and the case is remanded for further proceedings not inconsistent with this opinion.

Pursuant to this Court's Rule 45.2, the Clerk is directed to issue the mandate in this case forthwith.

It is so ordered.

CHIEF JUSTICE REHNQUIST, with whom JUSTICE SCALIA and JUSTICE THOMAS join, concurring.

We join the *per curiam* opinion. We write separately because we believe there are additional grounds that require us to reverse the Florida Supreme Court's decision.

I

We deal here not with an ordinary election, but with an election for the President of the United States. In *Burroughs v. United States,* 290 U. S. 534, 545 (1934), we said:

"While presidential electors are not officers or agents of the federal government (In re Green, 134 U. S. 377, 379 [(1890)]), they exercise federal functions under, and discharge duties in virtue of authority conferred by, the Constitution of the United States. The President is vested with the executive power of the nation. The importance of his election and the vital character of its relationship to and effect upon the welfare and safety of the whole people cannot be too strongly stated."

Likewise, in *Anderson v. Celebrezze,* 460 U. S. 780, 794795 (1983) (footnote omitted), we said: "[I]n the context of a Presidential election, state-imposed restrictions implicate a uniquely important national interest. For the President and the Vice President of the United States are the only elected officials who represent all the voters in the Nation."

In most cases, comity and respect for federalism compel us to defer to the decisions of state courts on issues of state law. That practice reflects our understanding that the decisions of state courts are definitive pronouncements of the will of the States as sovereigns. Cf. *Erie R. Co. v. Tompkins,* 304 U. S. 64 (1938). Of course, in ordinary cases, the distribution of powers among the branches of a State's government raises no questions of federal constitutional law, subject to the requirement that the government be republican in character. See U. S. Const., Art. IV; § 4. But there are a few exceptional cases in which the Constitution imposes a duty or confers a power on a particular branch of a State's government. This is one of them. Article II,

§ 1, cl. 2, provides that "[e]ach State shall appoint, in such Manner as the *Legislature* thereof may direct," electors for President and Vice President. (Emphasis added.) Thus the text of the election law itself, and not just its interpretation by the courts of the States, takes on independent significance.

In *McPherson v. Blacker,* 146 U. S. 1 (1892), we explained that Art. II, § 1, cl. 2, "convey[s] the broadest power of determination" and "leaves it to the legislature exclusively to define the method" of appointment. 146 U. S., at 27. A significant departure from the legislative scheme for appointing Presidential electors presents a federal constitutional question.

Title 3 U. S. C. § 5 informs our application of Art. II, § 1, cl. 2, to the Florida statutory scheme, which, as the Florida Supreme Court acknowledged, took that statute into account. Section 5 provides that the State's selection of electors "shall be conclusive, and shall govern in the counting of the electoral votes" if the electors are chosen under laws enacted prior to election day, and if the selection process is completed six days prior to the meeting of the electoral college. As we noted in *Bush v. Palm Beach County Canvassing Bd., ante,* at 78:

> "Since § 5 contains a principle of federal law that would assure finality of the State's determination if made pursuant to a state law in effect before the election, a legislative wish to take advantage of the 'safe harbor' would counsel against any construction of the Election Code that Congress might deem to be a change in the law."

If we are to respect the legislature's Article II powers, therefore, we must ensure that postelection state-court actions do not frustrate the legislative desire to attain the "safe harbor" provided by § 5.

In Florida, the legislature has chosen to hold statewide elections to appoint the State's 25 electors. Importantly, the legislature has delegated the authority to run the elections and to oversee election disputes to the Secretary of State (Secretary), Fla. Stat. Ann. § 97.012(1) (Supp. 2001), and to state circuit courts, §§ 102.168(1), 102.168(8). Isolated sections of the code may well admit of more than one interpretation, but the general coherence of the legislative scheme may not be altered by judicial interpretation so as to wholly change the statutorily provided apportionment of responsibility among these various bodies. In any election but a Presidential election, the Florida Supreme Court can give as little or as much deference to Florida's executives as it chooses, so far as Article II is concerned, and this Court will have no cause to question the court's actions. But, with respect to a Presidential election, the court must be both mindful of the legislature's role under Article II in choosing the manner of appointing electors and deferential to those bodies expressly empowered by the legislature to carry out its constitutional mandate.

In order to determine whether a state court has infringed upon the legislature's authority, we necessarily must examine the law of the State as it existed prior to the action of the court. Though we generally defer to state courts on the interpretation of state law-see, e. g., *Mullaney v. Wilbur,* 421 U. S. 684 (1975)-there are of course areas in which the Constitution requires this Court to undertake an independent, if still deferential, analysis of state law.

For example, in *NAACP v. Alabama ex rel. Patterson,* 357 U. S. 449 (1958), it was argued that we were without jurisdiction because the petitioner had not pursued the correct appellate remedy in Alabama's state courts. Petitioner had sought a state-law writ of certiorari in the Alabama Supreme Court when a writ of mandamus, according to that court, was proper. We found this state-law ground inadequate to defeat our jurisdiction because we were "unable to reconcile the procedural holding of the Alabama Supreme Court" with prior Alabama precedent. *Id.,* at 456. The purported state-law ground was so novel, in our independent estimation, that "petitioner could not fairly be deemed to have been apprised of its existence." *Id.,* at 457.

Six years later we decided *Bouie v. City of Columbia, 378* U. S. 347 (1964), in which the state court had held, contrary to precedent, that the state trespass law applied to black sit-in demonstrators who had consent to enter private property but were then asked to leave. Relying upon NAACp, we concluded that the South Carolina Supreme Court's interpretation of a state penal statute had impermissibly broadened the scope of that statute beyond what a fair reading provided, in violation of due process. See 378 U. S., at 361362. What we would do in the present case is precisely parallel: hold that the Florida Supreme Court's interpretation of the Florida election laws impermissibly distorted them beyond what a fair reading required, in violation of Article 11.[1]

This inquiry does not imply a disrespect for state *courts* but rather a respect for the constitutionally prescribed role of state *legislatures.* To attach definitive weight to the pronouncement of a state court, when the very question at issue is whether the court has actually departed from the statutory meaning, would be to abdicate our responsibility to enforce the explicit requirements of Article II.

II

Acting pursuant to its constitutional grant of authority, the Florida Legislature has created a detailed, if not perfectly crafted, statutory scheme that provides for appointment of Presidential electors by direct election. Fla. Stat. Ann. § 103.011 (1992). Under the statute, "[v]otes cast for the actual candidates for President and Vice President shall be counted as votes cast for the presidential electors supporting such candidates." *Ibid.* The legislature has designated the Secretary as the "chief election officer," with the responsibility to "[o]btain and maintain uniformity in the application, operation, and interpretation of the election laws." Fla. Stat. Ann. § 97.012 (Supp. 2001). The state legislature has delegated to county canvassing boards the duties of administering elections. § 102.141. Those boards are responsible for providing results to the state Elections Canvassing Commission, comprising the Governor, the Secretary of State, and the Director of the Division of Elections. § 102.111. Cf. *Boardman v. Esteva,* 323 So. 2d 259, 268, n. 5 (1975) ("The election process ... is committed to the executive branch of government through duly designated officials all charged with specific duties .... [The] judgments [of these officials] are entitled to be regarded by the courts as presumptively correct ... ").

After the election has taken place, the canvassing boards receive returns from precincts, count the votes, and in the event that a candidate was defeated by 0.5% or less, conduct a mandatory recount. Fla. Stat. Ann. § 102.141(4) (Supp. 2001). The county canvassing boards must file certified election returns with the Department of State by 5 p.m. on the seventh day following the election.

§ 102.112(1). The Elections Canvassing Commission must then certify the results of the election. § 102.111(1).

The state legislature has also provided mechanisms both for protesting election returns and for contesting certified election results. Section 102.166 governs protests. Any protest must be filed prior to the certification of election results by the county canvassing board. § 102.166(4)(b). Once a protest has been filed, "[t]he county canvassing board may authorize a manual recount." § 102.166(4)(c). If a sample recount conducted pursuant to § 102.166(5) "indicates an error in the vote tabulation which could affect the outcome of the election," the county canvassing board is instructed to: "(a) Correct the error and recount the remaining precincts with the vote tabulation system; (b) Request the Department of State to verify the tabulation software; or (c) Manually recount all ballots," § 102.166(5). In the event a canvassing board chooses to conduct a manual recount of all ballots, § 102.166(7) prescribes procedures for such a recount.

Contests to the certification of an election, on the other hand, are controlled by § 102.168. The grounds for contesting an election include "[r]eceipt of a number of illegal votes or rejection of a number of legal votes sufficient to change or place in doubt the result of the election." § 102.168(3)(c). Any contest must be filed in the appropriate Florida circuit court, § 102.168(1), and the canvassing board or election board is the proper party defendant, § 102.168(4). Section 102.168(8) provides that "[t]he circuit judge to whom the contest is presented may fashion such orders as he or she deems necessary to ensure that each allegation in the complaint is investigated, examined, or checked, to prevent or correct any alleged wrong, and to provide any relief appropriate under such circumstances." In Presidential elections, the contest period necessarily terminates on the date set by 3 U. S. C. § 5 for concluding the State's "final determination" of election controversies.

In its first decision, *Palm Beach Canvassing Bd. v. Harris,* 772 So. 2d 1220 (2000) (*Harris I*), the Florida Supreme Court extended the 7-day statutory certification deadline established by the legislature.[2] This modification of the code, by lengthening the protest period, necessarily shortened the contest period for Presidential elections. Underlying the extension of the certification deadline and the shortchanging of the contest period was, presumably, the clear implication that certification was a matter of significance:

The certified winner would enjoy presumptive validity, making a contest proceeding by the losing candidate an uphill battle. In its latest opinion, however, the court empties certification of virtually all legal consequence during the contest, and in doing so departs from the provisions enacted by the Florida Legislature.

The court determined that canvassing boards' decisions regarding whether to recount ballots past the certification deadline (even the certification deadline established by *Harris I*) are to be reviewed *de novo,* although the Election Code clearly vests discretion whether to recount in the boards, and sets strict deadlines subject to the Secretary's rejection of late tallies and monetary fines for tardiness. See Fla. Stat. Ann. § 102.112 (Supp. 2001). Moreover, the Florida court held that all late vote tallies arriving during the contest period should be automatically included in the certification regardless of the certification deadline (even the certification deadline established by *Harris I*), thus virtually eliminating both the deadline and the Secretary's discretion to disregard recounts that violate it.[3]

Moreover, the court's interpretation of "legal vote," and hence its decision to order a contest-period recount, plainly departed from the legislative scheme. Florida statutory law cannot reasonably be thought to *require* the counting of improperly marked ballots.

Each Florida precinct before election day provides instructions on how properly to cast a vote, Fla. Stat. Ann. § 101.46 (1992); each polling place on election day contains a working model of the voting machine it uses, Fla. Stat. Ann. § 101.5611 (Supp. 2001); and each voting booth contains a sample ballot, § 101.46. In precincts using punchcard ballots, voters are instructed to punch out the ballot cleanly:

"AFTER VOTING, CHECK YOUR BALLOT CARD TO BE SURE YOUR VOTING SELECTIONS ARE CLEARLY AND CLEANLY PUNCHED AND THERE ARE NO CHIPS LEFT HANGING ON THE BACK OF THE CARD." Instructions to Voters, quoted in Brief for Respondent Harris et al. 13, n. 5.

No reasonable person would call it "an error in the vote tabulation," Fla. Stat. Ann. § 102.166(5) (Supp. 2001), or a "rejection of ... legal votes," § 102.168(3)(c),[4] when electronic or electromechanical equipment performs precisely in the manner designed, and fails to count those ballots that are not marked in the manner that these voting instructions explicitly and prominently specify. The scheme that the Florida Supreme Court's opinion attributes to the legislature is one in which machines are *required* to be "capable of correctly counting votes," § 101.5606(4), but which nonetheless regularly produces elections in which legal votes are predictably not tabulated, so that in close elections manual recounts are regularly required. This is of course absurd. The Secretary, who is authorized by law to issue binding interpretations of the Election Code, §§ 97.012,106.23, rejected this peculiar reading of the statutes. See DE 00-13 (opinion of the Division of Elections). The Florida Supreme Court, although it must defer to the Secretary's interpretations, see *Krivanek v. Take Back Tampa Political Committee, 625* So. 2d 840, 844 (Fla. 1993), rejected her reasonable interpretation and embraced the peculiar one. See *Palm Beach County Canvassing Bd. v. Harris,* 772 So. 2d 1273 (2000) (*Harris III*).

But as we indicated in our remand of the earlier case, in a Presidential election the clearly expressed intent of the legislature must prevail. And there is no basis for reading the Florida statutes as requiring the counting of improperly marked ballots, as an examination of the Florida Supreme Court's textual analysis shows. We will not parse that analysis here, except to note that the principal provision of the Election Code on which it relied, § 101.5614(5), was, as Chief Justice Wells pointed out in his dissent in *Gore v. Harris,* 772 So. 2d 1243, 1267 (2000) (*Harris II*), entirely irrelevant. The State's Attorney General (who was supporting the Gore challenge) confirmed in oral argument here that never before the present election had a manual recount been conducted on the basis of the contention that "undervotes" should have been examined to determine voter intent. Tr. of Oral Arg. in *Bush v. Palm Beach County Canvassing Bd.*, O. T. 2000, No. 00-836, pp. 39-40; cf. *Broward County Canvassing Board v. Hogan*, 607 So. 2d 508, 509 (Fla. Ct. App. 1992) (denial of recount for failure to count ballots with "hanging paper chads"). For the court to step away from this established practice, prescribed by the Secretary, the state official charged by the legislature with "responsibility to ... [o]btain and maintain uniformity in the application, operation, and interpretation of the election laws," § 97.012(1), was to depart from the legislative scheme.

III

The scope and nature of the remedy ordered by the Florida Supreme Court jeopardizes the "legislative wish" to take advantage of the safe harbor provided by 3 U. S. C. § 5. *Bush v. Palm Beach County Canvassing Bd., ante*, at 78 (*per curiam*). December 12, 2000, is the last date for a final determination of the Florida electors that will satisfy § 5. Yet in the late afternoon of December 8th-four days before this deadline-the Supreme Court of Florida ordered recounts of tens of thousands of so-called "undervotes" spread through 64 of the State's 67 counties. This was done in a search for elusive-perhaps delusive-certainty as to the exact count of 6 million votes. But no one claims that these ballots have not previously been tabulated; they were initially read by voting machines at the time of the election, and thereafter reread by virtue of Florida's automatic recount provision. No one claims there was any fraud in the election. The Supreme Court of Florida ordered this additional recount under the provision of the Election Code giving the circuit judge the authority to provide relief that is "appropriate under such circumstances." Fla. Stat. Ann. § 102.168(8) (Supp. 2001).

Surely when the Florida Legislature empowered the courts of the State to grant "appropriate" relief, it must have meant relief that would have become final by the cutoff date of 3 U. S. C. § 5. In light of the inevitable legal challenges and ensuing appeals to the Supreme Court of Florida and petitions for certiorari to this Court, the entire recounting process could not possibly be completed by that date. Whereas the majority in the Supreme Court of Florida stated its confidence that "the remaining undervotes in these counties can be [counted] within the required time frame," 772 So. 2d, at 1262, n. 22, it made no assertion that the seemingly inevitable appeals could be disposed of in that time. Although the Florida Supreme Court has on occasion taken over a year to resolve disputes over local elections, see, *e. g., Beckstrom v. Volusia County Canvassing Bd.,* 707 So. 2d 720 (1998) (resolving contest of sheriff's race 16 months after the election), it has heard and decided the appeals in the present case with great promptness. But the federal deadlines for the Presidential election simply do not permit even such a shortened process.

As the dissent noted:

"In [the four days remaining], all questionable ballots must be reviewed by the judicial officer appointed to discern the intent of the voter in a process open to the public. Fairness dictates that a provision be made for either party to object to how a particular ballot is counted. Additionally, this short time period must allow for judicial review. I respectfully submit this cannot be completed without taking Florida's presidential electors outside the safe harbor provision, creating the very real possibility of disenfranchising those nearly six million voters who are able to correctly cast their ballots on election day." 772 So. 2d, at 1269 (opinion of Wells, C. J.) (footnote omitted).

The other dissenters echoed this concern: "[T]he majority is departing from the essential requirements of the law by providing a remedy which is impossible to achieve and which will ultimately lead to chaos." *Id.,* at 1273 (Harding, J., dissenting, joined by Shaw, J.).

Given all these factors, and in light of the legislative intent identified by the Florida Supreme Court to bring Florida within the "safe harbor" provision of 3 U. S. C. § 5, the remedy prescribed by the Supreme Court of Florida cannot be deemed an "appropriate" one as of December 8. It significantly departed from the statutory framework in place on November 7, and authorized open-ended further proceedings which could not be completed by December 12, thereby preventing a final determination by that date.

For these reasons, in addition to those given in the *per* curiam opinion, we would reverse.

1. What is the basis of this case, and how does it relate to the Electoral College?

2. What past precedent was this opinion based on? What does that tell us about the way the Electoral College has been framed in the courts?

BACA, ET AL. V. HICKENLOOPER, ET AL., FROM UNITED STATES COURT OF APPEALS FOR THE 10TH CIRCUIT, DECEMBER 12, 2016

Plaintiffs/appellants Polly Baca and Robert Nemanich have filed an emergency motion for injunction pending appeal. For the reasons outlined below, we deny their motion.

I

COLORADO'S PRESIDENTIAL ELECTORS STATUTE

Colorado's Presidential Electors statute, Colo. Rev. Stat. 1-4-304, provides as follows:

(1) The presidential electors shall convene at the capital of the state, in the office of the governor at the capitol building, on the first Monday after the second Wednesday in the first December following their election at the hour of 12 noon and take the oath required by law for presidential electors.If any vacancy occurs in the office of a presidential elector because of death, refusal to act, absence, or other cause, the presidential electors present shall immediately proceed to fill the vacancy in the electoral college. When all vacancies have been filled, the presidential electors shall proceed to perform the duties required of them by the constitution and laws of the United States. The vote for president and vice president shall be taken by open ballot.

(2) The secretary of state shall give notice in writing to each of the presidential electors of the time and place of the meeting at least ten days prior to the meeting.

(3) The secretary of state shall provide the presidential electors with the necessary blanks, forms, certificates, or other papers or documents required to enable them to properly perform their duties.

(4) If desired, the presidential electors may have the advice of the attorney general of the state in regard to their official duties.

(5) Each presidential elector shall vote for the presidential candidate and, by separate ballot, vice-presidential candidate who received the highest number of votes at the preceding general election in this state.

Colo. Rev. Stat. § 1-4-304.

PLAINTIFFS/APPELLANTS

Baca is a resident of the City and County of Denver, Colorado. Nemanich is a resident of El Paso County, Colorado. Both Baca and Nemanich were nominated at the Democratic Convention on April 16, 2016, to be Presidential Electors for the State of Colorado. Both were required to sign affidavits at that time affirming that they would cast their ballots on December 19, 2016, for the Democratic Presidential and Vice-Presidential candidates.

Baca and Nemanich concede that the Democratic candidates for President and Vice-President, Hillary Clinton and Timothy Kaine, received the highest number of votes in the State of Colorado during the general election held on November 8, 2016. Baca and Nemanich also concede that, given these election results, Colo. Rev. Stat. § 1-4-304(5) mandates that they cast their votes for Clinton and Kaine.

Baca and Nemanich allege, however, that they "cannot be constitutionally compelled to vote for" Clinton and Kaine, and are instead "entitled to exercise their judgment and free will to vote for whomever they believe to be the most qualified and fit for the offices of President and Vice President." Complaint at 4. "For example," they allege, they "may vote for a consensus candidate, other than Clinton or Trump, upon whom electors from both parties and along the ideological spectrum can agree, so as to prevent" the Republican Presidential and Vice-Presidential Candidates, Donald Trump and Michael Pence, "from ascending to the highest offices in the United States." *Id.*

THE COLORADO SECRETARY OF STATE'S RESPONSE

On or about November 18, 2016, Nemanich contacted Colorado's Secretary of State, Wayne Williams, and asked "what would happen if" a Colorado state elector "didn't vote for . . . Clinton and . . . Kaine." *Id.*, Att. 1 at 7 (Nemanich Affidavit at 3).Williams responded, by email, saying that "if an elector failed to follow th[e] requirement" outlined in Colo. Rev. Stat. § 1-4-304(5), his "office would likely remove the elector and seat a replacement elector until all nine electoral votes were cast for the winning candidates." *Id.* at 9.

In recent days, Williams has allegedly instituted a new oath to be given to Colorado's Electors on December

19, 2016, and has stated that if an elector violates Colo.Rev. Stat. § 1-4-304(5), they will likely face either a misdemeanor or felony perjury charge.

PLAINTIFFS' INITIATION OF THIS ACTION

On December 6, 2016, plaintiffs initiated this action by filing a verified complaint against three Colorado state officials: Governor John Hickenlooper, Jr., Attorney General Cynthia Coffman, and Secretary of State Wayne Williams. The complaint alleged, in pertinent part, that Colo. Rev. Stat. § 1-4-304(5) violates Article II of the United States Constitution, as amended by the Twelfth Amendment, and compels speech in violation of the First Amendment.

On that same date, plaintiffs also filed a motion for temporary restraining order and preliminary injunction. They alleged in their motion that they were "substantially likely to prevail on the paramount issue that Colorado's elector binding statute, [Colo.Rev. Stat.] § 1-4-304(5), is unconstitutional because it violates Article II of the U.S.Constitution, as amended by the Twelfth Amendment, and it compels speech in violation of the First Amendment." Dist. Ct. Docket No. 2 at 4. They asked for an order declaring Colo. Rev. Stat. § 1-4-304(5) unconstitutional. They also asked for an order "temporarily and preliminarily enjoining and restraining Defendants . . . from removing or replacing[them] as electors, compelling them to vote for certain candidates, precluding them from voting for any candidates, or otherwise interfering with the vote of the electors on December 19, 2016." *Id.* at 14.

THE DISTRICT COURT'S DENIAL OF PLAINTIFFS' MOTION

On December 12, 2016, the district court held a hearing on plaintiffs' motion and,at the conclusion of the hearing, orally denied the motion. In doing so, the district court concluded that plaintiffs failed to establish a substantial likelihood of success on the merits of their claims. The district court also concluded that "granting an injunction would irreparably harm the status quo and the public's general expectations." Dist. Ct.Docket No. 23 at 68. Further, with respect to the balance of harms, the district court found that "the last-minute nature of this action . . . tip[ped] the scales in favor of the defendants rather than the plaintiff[s]." *Id.* at 69. Relatedly, the district court concluded that the public's interest "in fair and effective elections, political stability, [and the]legitimacy of the eventual winner . . . would be adversely affected if [it] granted this injunction." *Id.* at 70. Indeed, the district court concluded that granting the injunction"would undermine the electoral process and unduly prejudice the American people by prohibiting a successful transition of power." *Id.*

PLAINTIFFS' APPEAL

Plaintiffs filed a notice of appeal on December 13, 2016, and have since filed with this court their emergency motion for injunction pending appeal.

II

The issuance of an injunction pending appeal unquestionably amounts to"extraordinary relief." *Hobby Lobby*

Stores, Inc. v. Sebelius, — U.S. —, 136 S. Ct. 641,643 (2012); *see Ruckelshaus v. Monsanto Co.*, 463 U.S. 1315, 1316 (1983) (holding that "a stay pending appeal" will be granted "only under extraordinary circumstances"). "Inruling on . . . a request" for injunction pending appeal, "this court makes the same inquiry as it would when reviewing a district court's grant or denial of a preliminary injunction." *Homans v. City of Albuquerque*, 264 F.3d 1240, 1243 (10th Cir. 2001). Thus, the applicant must establish (1) "the likelihood of success on appeal," (2) "the threat of irreparable harm if the stay or injunction is not granted," (3) "the absence of harm to opposing parties if the stay or injunction is granted," and (4) that the public interest will not be harmed if the stay or injunction is granted. *Id.*

As discussed below, we conclude, after considering these four factors in light of the preliminary record before us, that the district court did not "abuse[] its discretion" in denying plaintiffs' motion for temporary restraining order and preliminary injunction and that plaintiffs have not "demonstrated a clear and unequivocal right to relief." *Id.*

LIKELIHOOD OF SUCCESS ON APPEAL

In analyzing plaintiffs' likelihood of success on appeal, we begin by addressing defendants' assertion that plaintiffs lack standing. We then turn to the question of whether plaintiffs have established a likelihood of success on appeal on their claims that Colo. Rev. Stat. § 1-4-304(5) violates Article II and the Twelfth Amendment of the United States Constitution, and the First Amendment of the United States Constitution.

A) PLAINTIFFS' STANDING

Defendants argue that plaintiffs are, in essence, state officials who lack Article III standing to challenge the constitutionality of a state statute. In support, they cite primarily to the Supreme Court's decision in *Columbus & Greenville Ry. v. Miller*, 283U.S. 96, 99-100 (1931). We are not persuaded, however, that *Columbus* necessarily leads to the conclusion that the plaintiffs in this case lack standing. *Columbus* involved a challenge by a state tax collector to the validity of a state tax law. Notably, the taxpayer in *Columbus*, i.e., the party directly affected by the state tax law, conceded the validity of the law. In the instant case, in contrast, plaintiffs allege that Colo. Rev. Stat. § 1-4-304(5) infringes upon their own personal constitutional rights. At this stage of the proceedings, and given the preliminary record before us, we conclude that is sufficient to provide them with standing to challenge Colo. Rev. Stat. § 1-4-304(5). *See Coleman v. Miller*, 30 U.S.433, 438 (1939) (holding that state legislators had standing to restrain action on a resolution, as they had "a plain, direct and adequate interest in maintaining the effectiveness of their votes").

B) THE ARTICLE II AND TWELFTH AMENDMENT CLAIM

As noted, plaintiffs argue that Colo. Rev. Stat. § 1-4-304(5) violates Article II, as amended by the Twelfth Amendment, by requiring electors to vote for the presidential and vice-presidential candidates who received the highest number of votes in the State of Colorado during the general election.

In addressing this argument, we begin by examining the relevant provisions of the Constitution.

The Constitution mandates that the election of the President of the United States occur by way of the Electoral College, rather than by individual voters at the general election, and it outlines both how the Electoral College is to be created and how it shall operate. In particular, Article II Section 1 of the Constitution provides, in pertinent part:

> Each State shall appoint, in such Manner as the Legislature thereof may direct, a Number of Electors, equal to the whole Number of Senators and Representatives to which the State may be entitled in the Congress; but no Senator or Representative, or Person holding an Office of Trust or Profit under the United States, shall be appointed an Elector.
>
> * * *
>
> The Congress may determine the Time of chusing the Electors, and the Day on which they shall give their Votes; which Day shall be the same throughout the United States.

U.S. Const. art. II, § 1.[1]

As originally established, Article II section I also addressed the details of how Electors would cast their votes and how those votes would be counted. That language was superseded by the Twelfth Amendment to the Constitution, which was ratified on June 15, 1804. The Twelfth Amendment provides, in pertinent part:

> The Electors shall meet in their respective states, and vote by ballot for President and Vice President, one of whom, at least, shall not be an inhabitant of the same state with themselves; they shall name in their ballots the person voted for as President, and in distinct ballots the person voted for as Vice-President, and they shall make distinct lists of all persons voted for as President, and of all persons voted for as Vice-President, and of the number of votes for each, which lists they shall sign and certify, and transmit sealed to the seat of the government of the United States, directed to the President of the Senate;—The President of the Senate shall, in the presence of the Senate and House of Representatives, open all the certificates and the votes shall then be counted.;— The person having the greatest number of votes for President, shall be the President, if such number be a majority of the whole number of Electors appointed; and if no person have such majority, then from the persons having the highest numbers not exceeding three on the list of those voted for as President, the House of Representatives shall choose immediately, by ballot, the President. But in choosing the President, the votes shall be taken by states,the representation from each state having one vote; a quorum for this purpose shall consist of a member or members from two-thirds of the states,and a majority of all the states shall be necessary to a choice. * * * The person having the greatest number of votes as Vice-President, shall be Vice-President,

if such number be a majority of the whole number of Electors appointed, and if no person have a majority, then from the two highest numbers on the list, the Senate shall choose the Vice-President; a quorum for the purpose shall consist of two-thirds of the whole number of Senators, and a majority of the whole number shall be necessary to a choice. But no person constitutionally ineligible to the office of President shall be eligible to that of Vice-President of the United States.

U.S. Const. amend. XII.

Lastly, Section 3 of the Fourteenth Amendment addresses who may not serve as a State Elector:

No person shall be . . . [an] elector of President and Vice President . . .. who, having previously taken an oath, as a member of Congress, or as an officer of the United States, or as a member of any State legislature, or as an executive or judicial officer of any State, to support the Constitution of the United States, shall have engaged in insurrection or rebellion against the same or given aid or comfort to the enemies thereof.

U.S. Const. amend. XIV, § 3.

Plaintiffs argue that Colo. Rev. Stat. § 1-4-304(5) violates Article II and the Twelfth Amendment by rendering electors superfluous. In making this argument, however, plaintiffs fail to quote any of these provisions of the Constitution. And, more importantly, they fail to point to a single word in any of these provisions that support their position that the Constitution requires that electors be allowed the opportunity to exercise their discretion in choosing who to cast their votes for.[2] We conclude that this failure is fatal at this stage of the litigation. As noted, it is plaintiffs' burden to establish a likelihood of success on appeal. By failing to point us to any language in the Constitution that would support their position, we conclude they have failed to meet their burden.[3]

But even if we were to overlook the plaintiffs failure to point us to the Constitutional language that supports their position, they raise at best a debatable argument. Defendants point instead to the direction that: "Each State shall appoint, in such Manner as the Legislature thereof may direct, a Number of Electors . . . ." U.S.Const. Art. II, § 2. And they argue that the Supreme Court has held this power to be plenary under *McPherson v. Blacker*, 146 U.S. 1, 35-36 (1892). Accordingly, we cannot conclude the plaintiffs have met their burden of showing a likelihood of success on the merits.

Plaintiffs also argue that "[r]equiring an Elector to vote is clearly an improper qualification because it mandates that only the people that agree to vote for particular candidates are allowed (i.e., qualified) to become Electors." Emergency Motion at 7-8. We are not persuaded, however, that the requirement to vote consistent with the majority vote in the state is a "qualification." The term qualification suggests a preexisting condition or quality that either renders a person eligible or ineligible to be an Elector. *See* Oxford Dictionaries (defining qualification as "[a] quality or accomplishment that makes someone suitable for a particular job or activity"; "[a]

condition that must be fulfilled before a right can be acquired; an official requirement."). Under this definition, a pledge to vote for a particular candidate (like the ones that the plaintiffs in this case made to vote for the Democratic nominees for President and Vice-President) would be a qualification. But a statutory requirement to vote in a certain way, like the one in Colo. Rev. Stat. § 1-4-304(5), is more in the way of a duty than a qualification.

Lastly, plaintiffs argue that Colo. Rev. Stat. § 1-4-304(5) violates the Supremacy Clause by usurping Congress's exclusive power to count electoral votes. Emergency Motion at 12 (citing U.S. Const. amend. XII and 3 U.S.C. § 15). In support, plaintiffs argue that Colo. Rev. Stat. § 1-4-304(5) "gives Colorado the authority to discount/ delete/ignore an elector's vote for persons who did not win the popular vote in the state." *Id.* In turn, they argue that "[i]f Congress counts the votes, and it has counted over 150 'faithless' electors' votes over the centuries, the states lack the power to count an electors' [sic] vote," and thus "the statute is unconstitutional." *Id.*

The problem with this argument is that, according to the limited record before us, defendant Williams' threat to remove and place any elector who fails to comply with Colo. Rev. Stat. § 1-4-304(5) is not based on the text of that provision, but rather upon his interpretation of the authority afforded to him under Colo. Rev. Stat. § 1-4-304(1). As noted above, § 1-4-304(1) expressly affords the State of Colorado with authority to "fill [any] vacanc[ies] in the electoral college" prior to the start of voting. Whether that statute also affords the State with authority to remove an elector after voting has begun is not a question that has been posed by plaintiffs to either the district court or this court.[4]

C) THE FIRST AMENDMENT CLAIM

Plaintiffs also argue that Colo. Rev. Stat. § 1-4-304(5) violates their First Amendment rights by burdening their core political speech and compelling them to vote in a certain way. The problem for plaintiffs at this stage, however, is that they fail to identify any authority establishing, or even remotely suggesting, that the First Amendment applies to electors. *See Clark v. Cmty. for Creative Non-Violence*, 468 U.S.288, 293 n.5 (1984) (holding that "it is the obligation of the person desiring to engage in assertedly expressive conduct to demonstrate that the First Amendment even applies."). For these reasons, we conclude that plaintiffs have failed to establish a likelihood of success on the merits of the claims asserted in their appeal.

IRREPARABLE HARM

Plaintiffs argue that they will suffer irreparable harm if an injunction is not granted pending appeal. In support, they argue that, in light of defendant Williams' statements to date, there is a substantial likelihood that he will remove and replace them if they fail to vote for Clinton and Kaine. The problem with this argument is two-fold. First, as we have discussed, plaintiffs have failed to establish a likelihood of success on the merits of their constitutional challenges to Colo. Rev. Stat. § 1-4-304(5). In other words, they have failed at this point to establish that the State of Colorado cannot constitutionally require them to vote for Clinton and Kaine. Second, any removal and replacement authority that defendant Williams may possess derives not from § 1-4-304(5), but rather from § 1-4-304(1). While we question whether that subsection provides him any such authority after voting has commenced, that precise question is not before us.

Plaintiffs also argue that defendant Williams has threatened to charge them with a felony or misdemeanor if they fail to comply with § 1-4-304(5). The district court declined to address this argument because plaintiffs presented it for the first time at the hearing on their motion for temporary restraining order and preliminary injunction. Dist. Ct. Docket No. 23 at 66. We conclude that the district court did not abuse its discretion in this regard and thus adopt the same position.

HARM TO OPPOSING PARTIES IF THE INJUNCTION IS GRANTED

Plaintiffs argue that "[n]o hardship will occur to Defendants or the State if the injunction is implemented." Emergency Motion at 18. They explain that "[t]here will be no need to re-do the election" because when the people of Colorado "cast their ballots for presidential and vice-presidential candidates, they were voting for electors specific to political parties/candidates," and "[i]t is up to those electors, who have now been chosen by the people of Colorado, to choose the best candidates." *Id.* Further, they argue, the injunction would "not require Defendants to take any action," and would "merely prevent[] Defendants from enforcing an unconstitutional statute." *Id.* at 19.

The district court considered and rejected these very same arguments in denying plaintiffs' motion for temporary restraining order and preliminary injunction.

In doing so, it concluded that "the last-minute nature of this action, coupled with the potentially stifling effects it may have on our country, . . . tip[ped] the scales in favor of the defendants." Dist. Ct. Docket No. 66 at 69. We are unable to say that this amounted to an abuse of discretion, particularly given our conclusion that plaintiffs have failed to establish a likelihood of success on appeal.

PUBLIC INTEREST

Finally, plaintiffs argue that the public interest weighs in favor of granting the requested injunction because "[t]he public has a strong interest in the protection and enforcement of the rights established by the First and Fourteenth Amendments." Emergency Motion at 19. "The public," plaintiffs argue, also "has a strong interest in having the Electoral College operate as intended by deliberating and selecting a President and Vice-President who they believe best qualified." *Id.* Lastly, plaintiffs argue that "[t]he public has a significant interest in making sure fit and competent leaders are elected." *Id.*

The district court considered and rejected these same arguments, and instead concluded that granting plaintiffs' requested injunctive relief "would undermine the electoral process and unduly prejudice the American people by prohibiting a successful transition of power." Dist. Ct. Docket No. 66 at 70. We are unable to say that this amounted to an abuse of discretion, given plaintiffs' failure to establish a likelihood of prevailing on appeal.

III

Plaintiffs' emergency motion for injunction pending appeal is DENIED.

1. What is the relationship between the First Amendment and the Electoral College?

CHAPTER 4

WHAT THE ADVOCATES SAY

Advocacy groups play an important role in shaping our public debate about the Electoral College and in advancing legislative proposals to address the many questions we've already seen surrounding the role of the Electoral College in elections. The largest question regarding the Electoral College is whether it should be kept, and if not, should it be reformed or done away with completely. There are many competing answers to those questions, and for each there are strong legal, historical, and philosophical arguments both for and against. Groups like those below are crucial to understanding all of these sides, although it is important to remember that advocacy groups have a specific agenda and that their literature and research will likely skew toward their specific mission.

"KEEP THE ELECTORAL COLLEGE," BY LAWRENCE W. REED, FROM THE FOUNDATION FOR ECONOMIC EDUCATION, MARCH 1, 2001

Should the Electoral College be abolished? Last year's presidential election raised the question once again, but it also answered it with an emphatic NO! The framers of the Constitution knew precisely what they were doing when they established the system for electing presidents, which is more than anyone can say about the people who spent weeks last fall counting those celebrated dimpled and pregnant chads in Florida.

The 2000 election was the 53rd since George Washington was chosen in 1792. Even on the three previous occasions when a split decision between the popular and electoral votes occurred, the Electoral College was the mechanism for a decisive conclusion to an election. If popular votes alone determined the outcome, a dozen presidential elections would have been close enough for the result to be contested without end, or at least without an end that most Americans could see as fair and honest. What dragged out the contest between Bush and Gore were the partisan lawsuits and the tortuous methods employed to recount votes or decipher voter "intent."

Indeed, the closeness of the 2000 election in so many places—multiple states as well as the nation as a whole—suggests that we should thank our lucky stars the framers gave us the system we have.

It is precisely *because* of the Electoral College that the recounting of votes focused on one state instead of many. If the popular vote decided the winner, we would still be bogged down in questionable recounts in dozens, if not hundreds, of counties across the country. The potential for mistakes and abuse would have been enormously compounded, and the cloud over the eventual winner would have been all the more dark and ominous.

Some say that it is inherently unfair for a candidate to win in the Electoral College and become president if *another* candidate actually has more popular votes. It should be noted at the outset that it is extremely unlikely this could ever happen when the popular vote margin is wide. A narrow margin in the popular vote—narrow enough to be wiped out with a few vote-rigging recounts—cries out for a decisive conclusion, and that's what the Electoral College offers.

But whether the losing candidate's popular-vote victory is large or small, the fact that a win in the Electoral College is all that finally matters is not unfair. It's not unfair that little Delaware gets just as many senators as big California. It's not unfair that 34-year-olds can't become president or that a simple majority in the Congress is insufficient to approve a treaty, convict an impeached president, or amend the Constitution. Nor is it unfair that the winner of the World Series is the team that wins four games, not necessarily the one that has the most runs. These are the rules of the game, and in the case of the Electoral College, the rules were written for some very good reasons.

At the 1787 Constitutional Convention, some delegates wanted the popular vote to elect the president. Others argued that Congress should make the pick. The smaller, less populated states feared, correctly, that under either of those options they would be swallowed up or ignored by the larger, more populous states. The Electoral College represented not only a compromise to accommodate the concerns of the small states, but also a singular act of genius on the part of the framers. They did not reject the notion of a truly "democratic" election; they left the matter to the states. As it turned out, a democratic election determines each state's vote for president in the Electoral College. The institution serves as a pillar of our federal system of government, wherein the states—which created the central government in the first place—do not dissolve into an amorphous national mass but rather retain a substantial identity and hence a check on unbridled power in Washington.

Moreover, the fact that a candidate must win a majority in the Electoral College means that he cannot focus all his resources on only a few large states. He must fashion a truly national appeal, as opposed to a divisive regional one. That helps assure that the winner will enjoy an added measure of support and legitimacy that derives from a relatively broad base.

Thankfully, the question of abolishing the Electoral College is moot because the hurdles a constitutional amendment has to jump are simply too high. Too many small states would block it, as they have before.

One reform that does make sense is one requiring that electors vote for the candidate who won their respective states. The framers assumed that they would, but left it to the states to settle the details. Twenty-one jurisdictions (including the District of Columbia) have such a requirement, but 30 do not.

Finally, it may be instructive to everyone who followed the recent election controversy to consider a page from presidential history.

The last time a close election produced a split decision in the popular vote and the Electoral College was 1888. Grover Cleveland, the incumbent Democratic president, had been through a close one once before. In 1884, he won New York by just 1,200 votes—and with it, the presidency—but a switch of barely 600 votes in that one state alone would have swung the election to Republican James G. Blaine. Four years later, Cleveland bested Benjamin Harrison by about 100,000 votes out of 11 million cast nationwide but he lost in the Electoral College 233-168. Because the contest was tight in a number of states, a slight shift in the popular vote plurality would have easily won it all for the incumbent.

One reason the American people accepted the 1888 outcome was that the federal government was not so much a presence in their lives as today's government is in ours. Cut Washington down to its proper size, and who wins won't be of earthshaking consequence.

Cleveland handled his 1888 defeat with dignity—no recounts, no lawsuits, no spin. Alyn Brodsky, in his superb biography, *Grover Cleveland: A Study in Character*, records that when reporters asked to what he ascribed his defeat, Cleveland smiled and said, "It was mainly because the other party had the most votes." The "votes" to which he referred were the ones that really matter under the Constitution—*Electoral College* votes.

1. Why does the author support keeping the Electoral College?

2. How does he use history to back up his argument? Do you find it effective?

"ELECTORAL COLLEGE: IS IT TIME TO SHAKE UP THE SYSTEM?," BY WAYNE BAKER, FROM *READ THE SPIRIT: OUR VALUES*

The debate already is rising across the nation: Is it time to shake up the Electoral College?

Hundreds of news stories from NPR to newspapers are raising questions under headlines such as: "Is the Electoral College antiquated?" "Tampering with the Electoral College," and one recent Washington Post commentary headlined "Leave Bad Enough Alone."

Debates about our system of indirect election have arisen since the beginning when it was prescribed in the U.S. Constitution, as we will discuss in our series this week.

Today, I'd like to ask this fundamental question: Would you rather have the president elected by popular vote—that is, elected directly by the American people—or do you prefer the current indirect system, where voters elect electors who formally cast the vote?

Under the current system, the candidate who gets the most votes nationwide is not always the winner. This has happened three times so far: 1876, 1888, and 2000. The winners were all Republicans: Rutherford Hayes, Benjamin Harrison and George W. Bush. In each case, the winner received more electoral votes than his opponent, though the opponents received more votes cast by citizens. In the latest instance, many Democrats felt Bush "stole" the election, while many Republicans renewed their faith in the wisdom of the founding fathers to avoid direct democracy.

Almost every state operates with a winner-takes-all system. This means that the candidate with the most popular votes gets all electoral votes. All but two states—Maine and Nebraska—use this method. Maine and Nebraska use the Congressional District Method. This means that a candidate gets electoral votes proportionately, based on the popular vote in each state congressional district.

Today, there's a proposal to use this proportional method in Pennsylvania. If it had been used in 2008, McCain would have received 11 electoral votes to Obama's 10—even though Obama won the statewide popular vote by 10 points. Republicans who favor the change say it's a fairer system; opponents say it's just a Republican political ploy meant to get their candidate in office in 2012.

But the Pennsylvanian proposal still retains the Electoral College system.

1. Based on this article, do you feel this author supports or opposes the Electoral College? Why?

"THE PLAN," FROM EQUAL VOTES: ONE PERSON=ONE VOTE

THE PROBLEM WITH OUR PRESIDENTIAL ELECTIONS: OUR VOTES ARE NOT EQUAL

At the core of democracy lies a simple principle—that all votes should count equally. Whether you're white or black, rich or poor, from Rapid City, SD or Cedar Rapids, IA, your vote should count the same as the vote of anyone else. "One person, one vote!"

This principle is violated by the way we elect our president. Because of the winner-take-all system of allocating Electoral College votes, the only votes that count are those for the person who wins the state in which they were cast. In 2016, this resulted in over 52 million votes being ignored in the presidential election – that is hardly being counted equally.

All but two states (Maine & Nebraska) assign all their Electoral College votes to the winner of the popular vote in that state—regardless of the margin of victory. For example, in the last election:

- Hillary Clinton beat Donald Trump by just 45,000 votes in Minnesota, winning 46.4% to 44.9%. Yet she got 100% of Minnesota's 10 Electoral College votes, while Trump got zero.
- In Michigan, Trump beat Clinton by just 10,000 votes, but he got every single one of their 16 Electoral College votes, while she got zero.

This is the consequence of winner-take-all: the votes for president of millions of U.S. citizens get discarded, simply because they are not in the majority in a particular state.

THE RESULTS OF THIS INEQUALITY UNDERMINE OUR REPUBLIC

States originally adopted winner-take-all because it amplified the power of their votes. But once (practically) every other state had embraced winner-take-all, that effect was nullified, and presidential campaigns shifted their focus. Under winner-take-all, the only states in which it makes any sense for a presidential candidate to campaign are "battleground states"— states in which the popular vote can be expected to be so close that one side has a real chance to beat the other.

In 2016:

- Two-thirds of campaign events happened in just six battleground states—Florida, North Carolina, Ohio, Pennsylvania, Virginia, and Michigan.
- Four battleground states—Florida, North Carolina, Ohio and Pennsylvania—saw 71% of campaign ad spending and 57% of candidate appearances.
- The 14 battleground states saw 99% of ad spending and 95% of candidate campaign stops.

The consequence of this concentration for our democracy is profound. To get elected president, candidates must persuade not a majority of American voters, but a majority of voters in only 14 states.

Voters in battleground states tend to be whiter and older than Americans generally, so presidential platforms are skewed towards those populations. The issues that matter to younger Americans, and to people of color, are thus largely invisible (or hidden) in battleground campaigns. Winner-take-all in effect outsources the selection of the president to a fraction of America's voters (35% in 2016)—a fraction that does not in any sense represent the majority of America.

Even worse, these rules increase the probability of a "minority president"—a president who loses the popular vote, yet wins in the Electoral College. **Two of our last three presidents** have taken office after losing the popular vote, and that probability will likely increase over time.

THIS INEQUALITY IS NOT IN OUR CONSTITUTION

Contrary to what most people might think, the winner-take-all allocation of electoral votes is not in the Constitution. It was adopted by 48 states to give themselves more power in the presidential election.

It is time for the Supreme Court to end it. The Constitution, through the Electoral College, does create some inherent inequality. But that is no justification for allowing the states to create even more—especially when the consequence of that inequality is to systematically skew the focus of presidential campaigns. There is no good reason for this inequality. There is no democratic justification for it. It has made our presidential elections the least democratic of all our elections.

HERE'S OUR PLAN TO FIX THIS PROBLEM

Equal Votes is a crowdfunded legal challenge to the winner-take-all method for allocating Electoral College votes. Based on the "one person, one vote" principle already articulated by the Supreme Court in Bush v. Gore, we believe the winner-take-all system is unconstitutional—it is a violation of the Equal Protection Clause that ensures all of us, and all of our votes, must be treated equally under the law.

The claim we will make throughout this legal case is that by allocating their Electoral College votes according to winner-take-all, these states effectively discard the votes of United States citizens in the only meaningful count for electing the president—in the Electoral College.

We will ask those courts to apply the principle of "one person, one vote" to the winner-take-all system.

Our goal is to have our case heard in time for the 2020 election.

We've pulled together an all-star legal team, and together we've filed four lawsuits in four district courts on behalf of real voters affected by this system. We're representing plaintiffs in these four states whose votes for president are effectively discarded because the other party's candidate for president always, consistently, wins in their state.

To get this campaign going, we need your support. We have secured an initial commitment of pro bono legal work to enable us to launch this litigation project. But we will need to raise much more over the life of the litigation in order to win this case. Join us in this fight by contributing whatever you can, and by volunteering to help in whatever way you believe is best.

The most important part of this fight will come from the many people we hope to rally to equality: "one person, one vote." It's not just a principle of a fair democracy—it must also be the law.

1. What issues does Equal Votes raise regarding the Electoral College?

2. How do they seek to find solutions to these issues? Do they want to reform the Electoral College or get rid of it?

"IN DEFENSE OF THE ELECTORAL COLLEGE*," BY ALLEN GUELZO AND JAMES H. HULME, FROM *PICKING THE PRESIDENT: UNDERSTANDING THE ELECTORAL COLLEGE*, EDITED BY ERIC BURIN, 2017

There is hardly anything in the Constitution harder to explain, or easier to misunderstand, than the Electoral College. And when a presidential election hands the palm to a candidate who comes in second in the popular vote but first in the Electoral College tally, something deep in our democratic viscera balks and asks why the Electoral College shouldn't be dumped as a useless relic of 18th century white, gentry privilege.

Actually, there have been only five occasions when a closely divided popular vote and the electoral vote have failed to point in the same direction. No matter. After last week's results, we're hearing a litany of complaints: the Electoral College is undemocratic, the Electoral College is unnecessary, the Electoral College was invented to protect slavery — and the demand to push it down the memory hole.

All of which is strange because the Electoral College is at the core of our system of federalism. The Founders who sat in the 1787 Constitutional Convention lavished an extraordinary amount of argument on the Electoral College, and it was by no means one-sided. The great Pennsylvania jurist James Wilson believed that "if we are to establish a national Government," the president should be chosen by a direct, national vote of the people. But wise old Roger Sherman of Connecticut replied that the president ought to be elected by Congress, since he feared that direct election of presidents by the people would lead to the creation of a monarchy. "An independence of the Executive [from] the supreme Legislature, was in his opinion the very essence of tyranny if there was any such thing." Sherman was not trying to undermine the popular will, but to keep it from being distorted by a president who mistook popular election as a mandate for dictatorship.

Quarrels like this flared all through the convention, until, at almost the last minute, James Madison "took out a Pen and Paper, and sketched out a mode of Electing the President" by a "college" of "Electors ... chosen by those of the people in each State, who shall have the Qualifications requisite."

The Founders also designed the operation of the Electoral College with unusual care. The portion of Article 2, Section 1, describing the Electoral College is longer and descends to more detail than any other single issue the Constitution addresses. More than the federal judiciary — more than the war powers — more than taxation and representation. It prescribes in precise detail how "Each State shall appoint ... a Number of Electors, equal to the whole Number of Senators and Representatives to which the State may be entitled in the Congress"; how these electors "shall vote by Ballot" for a president and vice president; how they "shall sign and certify, and transmit sealed to the Seat of the Government of the United States, directed to the President of the Senate" the results of their balloting; how a tie vote must be resolved; what schedule the balloting should follow; and on and on.

Above all, the Electoral College had nothing to do with slavery. Some historians have branded the

Electoral College this way because each state's electoral votes are based on that "whole Number of Senators and Representatives" from each State, and in 1787 the number of those representatives was calculated on the basis of the infamous three-fifths clause. But the Electoral College merely reflected the numbers, not any bias about slavery (and in any case, the three-fifths clause was not quite as proslavery a compromise as it seems, since Southern slaveholders wanted their slaves counted as five-fifths for determining representation in Congress, and had to settle for a whittled-down fraction). As much as the abolitionists before the Civil War liked to talk about the "proslavery Constitution," this was more of a rhetorical posture than a serious historical argument. And the simple fact remains, from the record of the Constitutional Convention's proceedings (James Madison's famous Notes), that the discussions of the Electoral College and the method of electing a president never occur in the context of any of the convention's two climactic debates over slavery. If anything, it was the Electoral College that made it possible to end slavery, since Abraham Lincoln earned only 39 percent of the popular vote in the election of 1860, but won a crushing victory in the Electoral College. This, in large measure, was why Southern slaveholders stampeded to secession in 1860-61. They could do the numbers as well as anyone, and realized that the Electoral College would only produce more anti-slavery Northern presidents.

Yet, even on those terms, it is hard for Americans to escape the uncomfortable sense that, by inserting an extra layer of "electors" between the people and the president, the Electoral College is something less than democratic. But even if we are a democratic nation, that is not all we are. The Constitution also makes us a federal union, and the Electoral College is pre-eminently both the symbol and a practical implementation of that federalism.

The states of the union existed before the Constitution, and in a practical sense, existed long before the revolution. Nothing guaranteed that, in 1776, the states would all act together, and nothing that guaranteed that after the Revolution they might not go their separate and quarrelsome ways, much like the German states of the 18th century or the South American republics in the 19th century. The genius of the Constitutional Convention was its ability to entice the American states into a "more perfect union." But it was still a union of states, and we probably wouldn't have had a constitution or a country at all unless the route we took was federalism.

The Electoral College was an integral part of that federal plan. It made a place for the states as well as the people in electing the president by giving them a say at different points in a federal process and preventing big-city populations from dominating the election of a president.

Abolishing the Electoral College now might satisfy an irritated yearning for direct democracy, but it would also mean dismantling federalism. After that, there would be no sense in having a Senate (which, after all, represents the interests of the states), and further along, no sense even in having states, except as administrative departments of the central government. Those who wish to abolish the Electoral College ought to go the distance, and do away with the entire federal system and perhaps even retire the Constitution, since the federalism it was designed to embody would have disappeared.

None of that, ironically, is liable to produce a more democratic election system. There are plenty of democracies, like Great Britain, where no one ever votes directly for a head of the government. But more important, the Electoral College actually keeps presidential elections from going undemocratically awry because it makes unlikely the possibility that third-party candidates will garner enough votes to make it onto the electoral scoreboard.

Without the Electoral College, there would be no effective brake on the number of "viable" presidential candidates. Abolish it, and it would not be difficult to imagine a scenario where, in a field of a dozen micro-candidates, the "winner" only needs 10 percent of the vote, and represents less than 5 percent of the electorate. And presidents elected with smaller and smaller pluralities will only aggravate the sense that an elected president is governing without a real electoral mandate.

The Electoral College has been a major, even if poorly comprehended, mechanism for stability in a democracy, something which democracies are sometimes too flighty to appreciate. It may appear inefficient. But the Founders were not interested in efficiency; they were interested in securing "the blessings of liberty." The Electoral College is, in the end, not a bad device for securing that.

1. What do the authors argue Americans get wrong about the Electoral College?

2. According to the authors, why does the Electoral College remain important today?

CHAPTER 5

WHAT THE MEDIA SAY

The media is an invaluable resource for studying the Electoral College. It provides some of the most insightful analysis of the way the Electoral College functions in real time, and articles serve as concise ways to understand the many dynamics at play within the Electoral College debate. The media can also help us understand the ways in which the Electoral College intersects with other political or legal issues, deepening our sense of where the Electoral College sits within our democracy. Coverage of the Electoral College is an often more accessible window into how we think about the institution and process than academic or political publications, while maintaining the complexity of this historic body within our government. But that being said, coverage can be sparse due to the infrequent action taken by the Electoral College, which can create a sense that the issues surrounding the Electoral College are inadequately reported on outside of election cycles.

"DEMOCRACY OR REPUBLIC?," BY WALTER E. WILLIAMS, FROM THE FOUNDATION FOR ECONOMIC EDUCATION, JUNE 1, 2007

THE FOUNDING FATHERS INTENDED FOR THE UNITED STATES TO BE A REPUBLIC

How often do we hear the claim that our nation is a democracy? Was a democratic form of government the vision of the Founders? As it turns out, the word democracy appears nowhere in the two most fundamental founding documents of our nation—the Declaration of Independence and the Constitution. Instead of a democracy, the Constitution's Article IV, Section 4, declares "The United States shall guarantee to every State in this Union a Republican Form of Government." Our pledge of allegiance to the flag says not to "the democracy for which it stands," but to "the republic for which it stands." Is the song that emerged during the War of 1861 "The Battle Hymn of the Democracy" or "The Battle Hymn of the Republic"?

So what is the difference between republican and democratic forms of government? John Adams captured the essence of the difference when he said, "You have rights antecedent to all earthly governments; rights that cannot be repealed or restrained by human laws; rights derived from the Great Legislator of the Universe." Nothing in our Constitution suggests that government is a grantor of rights. Instead, government is envisioned as a protector of rights.

In recognition that it is government that poses the gravest threat to our liberties, the framers used negative phrases in reference to Congress throughout the first ten amendments to the Constitution, such as shall not abridge, infringe, deny, disparage, and shall not be violated, nor be denied. In a republican form of government, there is rule of law. All citizens, including government officials, are accountable to the same laws. Government power is limited and decentralized through a system of checks and balances. Government intervenes in civil society to protect its citizens against force and fraud, but does not intervene in the cases of peaceable, voluntary exchange.

Contrast the framers' vision of a republic with that of a democracy. According to Webster's dictionary, a democracy is defined as "government by the people; especially: rule of the majority." In a democracy the majority rules either directly or through its elected representatives. As in a monarchy, the law is whatever the government determines it to be. Laws do not represent reason. They represent power. The restraint is upon the individual instead of government. Unlike the rights envisioned under a republican form of government, rights in a democracy are seen as privileges and permissions that are granted by government and can be rescinded by government.

There is considerable evidence that demonstrates the disdain held by our founders for a democracy. James Madison, in Federalist No. 10, said that in a pure democracy, "there is nothing to check the inducement to sacrifice the weaker party or the obnoxious individual." At the 1787 Constitutional Convention, Edmund Randolph said, "that in tracing these evils to their origin every man had found it in the turbulence and follies of democracy." John Adams said, "Remember, democracy never lasts long. It soon wastes, exhausts, and murders itself. There was never a democracy yet that did not commit suicide." Later on, Chief Justice John Marshall observed, "Between a balanced republic and a democracy, the difference is like that between order and chaos." In a word or two, the Founders knew that a democracy would lead to the same kind of tyranny the colonies suffered under King George III.

The framers gave us a Constitution that is replete with anti-majority-rule, undemocratic mechanisms. One that has come in for frequent criticism and calls for elimination is the Electoral College. In their wisdom, the framers gave us the Electoral College so that in presidential elections large, heavily populated states could not use their majority to run roughshod over small, sparsely populated states. Amending the Constitution requires a two-thirds vote of both houses of Congress, or two-thirds of state legislatures, to propose an amendment and three-fourths of state legislatures to ratify it. Part of the reason for having a bicameral Congress is that it places another obstacle to majority rule. Fifty-one senators can block the wishes of 435 representatives and 49 senators. The Constitution gives the president a veto to thwart the power of all 535 members of Congress. It takes two-thirds of both houses of Congress to override the president's veto.

There is even a simpler way to expose the tyranny of majority rule. Ask yourself how many of your day-to-day choices would you like to have settled through the democratic process of majority rule. Would you want the kind of car you own to be decided through a democratic process, or would you prefer purchasing any car you please? Would like your choice of where to live, what clothes to purchase, what foods you eat, or what entertainment you enjoy to be decided through a democratic process?

I am sure that at the mere suggestion that these choices should be subject to a democratic vote, most of us would deem it a tyrannical attack on our liberties.

Most Americans see our liberties as protected by the Constitution's Bill of Rights, but that vision was not fully shared by its framers. In Federalist No. 84, Alexander Hamilton argued, "[B]ills of rights ... are not only unnecessary in the proposed Constitution, but would even be dangerous. For why declare that things shall not be done [by Congress] which there is no power to do? Why, for instance, should it be said that the liberty of the press shall not be restrained, when no power is given [to Congress] by which restrictions may be imposed?" James Madison agreed: "This is one of the most plausible arguments I have ever heard urged against the admission of a bill of rights into this system ... [because] by enumerating particular exceptions to the grant of power, it would disparage those rights which were not placed in that enumeration, and it might follow by implication, that those rights which were not singled out, were intended to be assigned into the hands of the general government, and were consequently insecure."

Madison thought this danger could be guarded against by the Ninth Amendment, which declares "The enumeration in the Constitution, of certain rights, shall not be construed to deny or disparage others retained by the people." Of course, the Ninth Amendment has little or no meaning in today's courts.

TRANSFORMED INTO A DEMOCRACY

Do today's Americans have contempt for the republican values laid out by our Founders, or is it simply a matter of our being unschooled about the differences between a republic and a democracy? It appears that most Americans, as well as their political leaders, believe that Congress should do anything it can muster a majority vote to do. Thus we have been transformed into a democracy. The most dangerous and insidious effect of majority rule is that it confers an aura of legitimacy, decency, and respectability on acts that would otherwise be deemed tyrannical. Liberty and democracy are not synonymous and could actually be opposites.

If we have become a democracy, I guarantee you that the Founders would be deeply disappointed by our betrayal of their vision. They intended, and laid out the ground rules for, a limited republican form of government that saw the protections of personal liberties as its primary function.

1. What does the author argue about the Founders' vision for American governance?

2. How does the Electoral College fit this vision or undermine it? Do you agree with the author's assessment?

"EXPERTS: CALL FOR ELECTORAL COLLEGE REVOLT UNLIKELY TO BE HEEDED IN STATE," BY AIDA CHAVEZ, FROM *CRONKITE NEWS*, DECEMBER 16, 2016

WASHINGTON — Death and taxes may be the only things certain in life, but the outcome of the Electoral College vote can't be far behind.

When Arizona's 11 presidential electors gather in Phoenix Monday to officially vote in the next president, experts say there is little chance that they will cast their ballots for anyone but President-elect Donald Trump, who won the popular vote in the state.

The Electoral College vote comes as just under 4.9 million people have signed a Change.org petition, the largest in that organization's history, urging electors to change their votes from Trump, whom the petition calls a "danger to the Republic."

Critics have called on electors to cast ballots instead for Democrat Hillary Clinton, who collected 2.5 million more votes than Trump, but lost the Electoral College by a large margin, one of just five candidates in history who have won the popular vote but not electoral vote.

But history and political pressure make it unlikely that electors will put Clinton in the White House.

"In the entire history of the Electoral College there have been 10 faithless electors, and two of them made a mistake," said Ray Haynes of National Popular Vote, an initiative to reform the Electoral College. "Only eight of them were actually faithless."

When voters went to the polls Nov. 8 they didn't actually elect the president – they elected the 538 members of the Electoral College who will do that job, one elector for every member of Congress and three for the District of Columbia. They are generally bound to vote for the candidate who won their state.

Although he lost the popular vote, Trump won enough states to amass 306 electoral votes, well over the 270 needed to win the presidency.

Arizona's 11 Electoral College members, chosen by the state's political party chairmen, will meet Dec. 19

at the State Capitol to cast their official votes for Trump. The state's electors include: GOP National Committeeman Bruce Ash, Walter Begay Jr., GOP National Committeewoman Sharon Giese, state party Chairman Robert Graham, state party Sergeant at Arms Alberto Gutier, Jerry Hayden, Carole Joyce, Jane Lynch, Foster Morgan, James O'Connor and Edward Robson.

Unlike many states that bind their electors to cast ballots for the winning ticket in the state, Arizona has no such law. But Jennifer Steen, associate research professor in political science at Arizona State University, said they probably don't need a law to bind them.

"Most of them are people who have been faithful to their political parties," Steen said. "The kind of people chosen to do this are chosen because they're loyal to their political party."

Repeated attempts to reach Arizona's electors were unsuccessful, including one who promptly hung up on a reporter.

Steen, who was a California presidential elector in 1996, said there was no such Electoral College drama then, after what she called an uncontroversial election.

"There was no talk of, 'What if I want to vote for somebody else?'" she said. "It was pretty routine."

While it is "more likely than normal" that this election put individuals in the Electoral College who "really don't like" Trump, Steen said that electors almost always vote for their pledged candidate.

"They're not bound by law, but they're bound by custom, by social convention," she said. "So for someone to break that, there will be social consequences and political consequences. They are risking their political allies ... although you never know when a maverick will get in there."

Haynes, noting that 38 electors would need to switch their votes to change the outcome of the race, said talk of Clinton supporters pressuring electors to change their vote is little more than a "silly political maneuver."

"It's a fun story without any substance at all," Haynes said. "The fact that it's getting any ink anywhere shows how little people know about the Electoral College."

1. What does it mean for Electoral College electors to revolt?

2. Why did state officials think such an event was unlikely?

"THE DEMOCRATS' BAD MAP," BY ALEC MACGILLIS, FROM *PROPUBLICA*, OCTOBER 22, 2016

HILLARY CLINTON LOOKS INCREASINGLY LIKELY TO WIN THE WHITE HOUSE, BUT HER PARTY FACES A BIG OBSTACLE TO SUCCESS IN CONGRESSIONAL RACES — DEMOCRATS ARE SORTING THEMSELVES INTO GEOGRAPHIC CLUSTERS WHERE MANY OF THEIR VOTES HAVE BEEN RENDERED ALL BUT SUPERFLUOUS.

Even as Hillary Clinton appears poised to win easily against a highly erratic candidate with a campaign in meltdown, a sobering reality awaits Democrats on Nov. 9. It seems likely that they will eke out at most a narrow majority in the Senate, but will fail to pick up the 30 seats they need to reclaim the House. If they do manage to win a Senate majority, it will be exceedingly difficult to hold it past 2018, when 25 of the party's seats must be defended, compared with eight Republican ones.

The Republican Party may seem in historic disarray, but it will most likely be able to continue to stymie the Democrats' legislative agenda, perpetuating Washington's gridlock for years to come.

Liberals have a simple explanation for this state of affairs: Republican-led gerrymandering, which has put Democrats at a disadvantage in the House and in many state legislatures. But this overlooks an even bigger problem for their party. More than ever, Democrats are sorting themselves into geographic clusters where many of their votes have been rendered all but superfluous, especially in elections for the Senate, House and state government.

This has long been a problem for the party, but it has grown worse in recent years. The clustering has economic and demographic roots, but also a basic cultural element: Democrats just don't want to live where they'd need to live to turn more of the map blue.

Americans' tendency toward political self-segregation has been underway for a while now — it's been eight years since Bill Bishop identified the dynamic in "The Big Sort." This helps explain why red-blue maps of so many states consist of dark-blue islands in the cities surrounded by red exurbs and rural areas, a distribution that is also driven by urban concentrations of racial minorities and by the decades-long shift in allegiance from Democratic to Republican among working-class white voters.

That hyper-concentration of Democratic votes has long hurt the party in the House and state legislatures. In Ohio, for instance, Republicans won 75 percent of the United States House seats in 2012 despite winning only 51 percent of the total votes for the House. That imbalance can be explained partly by Republican gerrymandering. But even if district lines were drawn in rational, nonpartisan ways, a disproportionate share of Democratic votes would still be clustered in urban districts, giving Republicans a larger share of seats than their share of the overall vote. Winning back control of state legislatures in Pennsylvania and Michigan could help Democrats in redistricting in 2020. But it would help more if their voters were not so concentrated in Philadelphia and Pittsburgh, Detroit and Ann Arbor.

"It would be awfully difficult to construct a map that wasn't leaning Republican," said the University of Michigan political scientist Jowei Chen. "Geography is just very unfortunate from the perspective of the Democrats."

More recently, a confluence of several trends has conspired to make the sorting disadvantageous for Democrats on an even broader scale — increasing the party's difficulties in House races while also affecting Senate elections and, potentially, future races for the presidency.

First, geographic mobility in the United States has become very class-dependent. Once upon a time, lower-income people were willing to pull up stakes and move to places with greater opportunity — think of the people who fled the Dust Bowl for California in the 1930s, or those who took the "Hillbilly Highway" out of Appalachia to work in Midwestern factories, or Southern blacks on the Great Migration. In recent decades, though, internal migration has slowed sharply, and the people who are most likely to move for better opportunities are the highly educated.

Second, higher levels of education are increasingly correlated with voting Democratic. This has been most starkly on display in the 2016 election, as polls suggest that Donald J. Trump may be the first Republican in 60 years to not win a majority of white voters with college degrees, even as he holds his own among white voters without degrees. But the trend of increasing Democratic identification among college graduates, and increasing Republican identification among non-graduates, was underway before Trump arrived on the scene. Today, Democrats hold a 12-point edge in party identification among those with a college degree or more. In 2004, the parties were even on that score.

Finally, in the United States the economic gap between the wealthiest cities and the rest of the country has grown considerably. The internet was supposed to allow wealth to spread out, since we could be connected anywhere — but the opposite has happened. Per capita income in the District of Columbia has gone from 29 percent above the United States average in 1980 to 68 percent in 2013; in the Bay Area, from 50 percent above to 88 percent; in New York City, from 80 percent above to 172 percent. Cities like New York, San Francisco, Seattle and Boston, exert a strong pull on mobile, highly educated, Democratic-leaning voters, while at the same time stirring resentment in the less prosperous areas those voters leave behind. And these economically dominant cities tend to be in deep-blue states.

How extreme is Democratic clustering? If you compare President Obama's 2012 performance with Al Gore's in 2000, you can see a huge increase in the Democratic percentage of the vote in the 68 largest metro areas. But it barely budged everywhere else. Some of that increase was caused by voters already in those cities flipping from Republican to Democratic. But it was also the gravitational effect.

This clustering of Democrats helps explain why Trump has been keeping it close in Ohio and Iowa, both states where some 72 percent of white residents over 24 lack college degrees, the highest share among the 13 most competitive states.

It works the other way in presidential elections, too. Democrats have gained in some other swing states with high levels of college-educated voters, like Virginia and Colorado, and they do at least reap a benefit in the Electoral College for having a lock on big states such as New York and California.

But it's another story in the Senate, where this dynamic helps explain why the Democrats are perpetually struggling to hold a majority. The Democrats have long been at a disadvantage in the Senate, where the populous, urbanized states where Democrats prevail get the same two seats as the rural states where Republicans are stronger. The 20 states where Republicans hold both Senate seats have, on average, 5.2 million people each; the 16 states where the Democrats hold both seats average 7.9 million people. Put another way, winning Senate elections in states with a total of 126 million people has netted the Democrats eight fewer seats than the Republicans get from winning states with 104 million people.

Clustering is part of the problem. All those Democrats gravitating to blue strongholds like New York and California get the party no more Senate seats than Republicans get from Idaho and from Wyoming, a state with a population of about 580,000, slightly more than Fresno, Calif. If the Democrats are going to gain a lasting hold on the Senate, they have to win seats in swing states. But that gets harder the more that Democratic-leaning voters flock to big, blue states, abandoning swing states like Ohio, where the Republican Rob Portman is gliding to re-election, or smaller red states where Democrats might still have a shot at holding Senate seats, like Montana, Indiana or North Dakota.

Jenn Topper has thought about this dynamic a lot, because she's a clear example of it. Topper, 31, grew up in Beavercreek, Ohio, a suburb of Dayton, a city that has lost nearly half its population since 1960. She left for college at Florida State, then for a public relations job in New York, then for a political communications job in Washington.

"When you grow up in Ohio, there's a bigger world out there, and if you know about it, you just want to go to it," she said.

A couple years ago, Topper and some colleagues who were also from Ohio were excited to meet "their" Democratic senator, Sherrod Brown, at an event. He asked them where they lived in Ohio. But they don't live in Ohio — and won't be able to vote for him in what is sure to be a tough race in 2018.

Topper's high school classmate Brett Stelter, 31, left Dayton after attending Ohio University. His father was a district parts manager for Honda, which has a plant near Dayton, and Stelter himself did part-time work at the plant. But his dream was to be an actor, and so he ended up in Los Angeles.

"There's just nothing to do in Ohio," he said. "The jobs are limited, but it's not just the jobs and the industries that are in Ohio, it's the mind-set that I didn't gravitate to."

Stelter, who voted twice for Obama, is disappointed that his vote is superfluous in California, and tries to make up for it by engaging on social media with people back home — people like his father, who is leaning toward Trump. "Part of me wishes I could be there to personally talk to people instead of trolling them on the internet," he said. But his political irrelevance is not enough to make him consider moving back. "Going back to Ohio to be able to vote every four years is not enough for me."

This clustering is happening even as many smaller cities and outlying regions are experiencing mini-cultural renaissances. For one thing, a foodie or beer snob now has much less to complain about when contemplating dining outside a big coastal city. And most of these places are much more affordable than Brooklyn or Los Angeles. But they can't seem to compare with the profusion of cool elsewhere.

Even cities making comebacks, with restored downtown buildings and plenty of locally brewed I.P.A., have the memory problem. If a city was on the ropes when young people left it, it's frozen in that form in their image of it. "You're competing with memory," Topper said. "People look back and remember what it was like when they were there. You don't often hear about how things are moving or growing or new things are happening. That picture of when you have left is all you have."

Of course, some people do go back. Brittney Vosters, 30, who went to high school and college in Dayton, left for several years, living in Chicago and enrolling in graduate school in public administration at Rutgers in New Jersey. She recently moved back to Cincinnati so her husband could go to graduate school in northern Kentucky. It has struck her how much her former Dayton classmates have sorted out politically. "It's noticeable that the people who left are more liberal-minded and the people who stayed are more Republican," she said.

And this sorting out is self-perpetuating, too. The fewer people you encounter of the opposite political persuasion, the more they become an unfathomable other, easily caricatured and impossible to find even occasional common ground with. By segregating themselves in narrow slices of the country, Democrats have also made it harder to make their own case. They are forever preaching to the converted, while their social distance also leaves them unprepared for what's coming from the other end of the spectrum. Changing that would mean adopting a broader notion of what it means to live in a happening place, and also exposing themselves to discomforts that most people naturally avoid, given the human tendency to seek out our own kind.

Vosters, for one, appreciates that her vote counts a lot more now in Ohio than it did when she was in New Jersey and Illinois. But she has no doubt where she'd like to end up for good. For her next move, she said, "I'd look at the political map and go toward the blue, because it's more comfortable to be around people who are like you."

1. How does clustering impact the Electoral College?

2. How can an issue like clustering be addressed?

CHAPTER 6

WHAT AVERAGE CITIZENS SAY

D espite the sometimes obscure nature of the Electoral College, it plays an important role in our democracy. The lives of citizens across the country are impacted by the Electoral College, and the issues at the heart of this debate are some of the most critical facing our country. As a result, there are many strongly held opinions about the future of the Electoral College among average citizens. Whether they favor tradition and maintaining the Electoral College or advocate for reforming or abolishing it, citizens are more and more in tune to what goes on within our political system, including during the Electoral College process.

"IN THE ELECTORAL COLLEGE WHITE VOTES MATTER MORE," BY LARA MERLING AND DEAN BAKER, FROM THE CENTER FOR ECONOMIC AND POLICY RESEARCH, NOVEMBER 13, 2016

For the second time in the last five elections we are seeing a situation where the candidate who came in second in the popular vote ends up in the White House. This is of course due to the Electoral College.

As just about everyone knows, the Electoral College can lead to this result since it follows a winner take all rule (with the exception of Nebraska and Maine). A candidate gets all the electoral votes of a state whether they win it by one vote or one million. In this election, Secretary Clinton ran up huge majorities in California and New York, but her large margins meant nothing in the Electoral College.

In addition to the problem of this winner take all logic, there is also the issue that people in large states are explicitly underrepresented in the Electoral College. While votes are roughly proportionately distributed, since even the smallest states are guaranteed three votes, the people in these states end up being over-represented in the Electoral College. For example, in Wyoming, there is an electoral vote for every 195,000 residents, in North Dakota there is one for every 252,000, and in Rhode Island one for every 264,000. On the other hand, in California there is an electoral vote for every 711,000 residents, in Florida one for every 699,000, and in Texas one for every 723,000.

The states that are overrepresented in the Electoral College also happen to be less diverse than the country as a whole. Wyoming is 84 percent white, North Dakota is 86 percent white, and Rhode Island is 74 percent white, while in California only 38 percent of the population is white, in Florida 55 percent, and in Texas 43 percent. White people tend to live in states where their vote counts more, and minorities in places where it counts less. This means that the Electoral College not only can produce results that conflict with a majority vote, but it is biased in a way that amplifies the votes of white people and reduces the voice of minorities.

ELECTORAL VOTES PER PERSON IN EACH GROUP

RELATIVE TO WHITE VOTERS

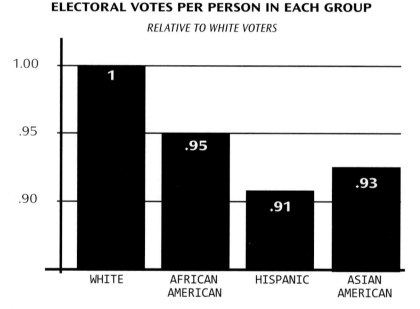

The figure illustrates the gap in Electoral College representation for minority voters. Based on the weight of each vote in each state and given the fact that most minority voters reside in states where each person's vote counts less in the Electoral College, the result is minority voters are grossly underrepresented. African American votes on average have a weight that is 95 percent as much as white votes, Hispanic votes are on average 91 percent, and Asian American votes, 93 percent as much of a white vote. In the Electoral College, white votes matter more.

ADDENDUM

It is worth noting that there is a fix to this problem which does not require a constitutional amendment or even action by Congress. The organization, National Popular Vote, has been pushing states to pass legislation whereby their electoral votes will go to the winner of the national popular vote. This switch does not happen until states representing a majority of electoral votes have passed the same legislation. At that point, the winner of the popular vote will automatically be the winner of the electoral vote.

1. According to the authors, how does race impact the Electoral College?

2. Do the authors identify any solutions to this issue?

"WHY HAVE AN ELECTORAL COLLEGE?," BY BERTEL SPARKS, FROM THE FOUNDATION FOR ECONOMIC EDUCATION, APRIL 1, 1969

This article is an uncle's response to a lad's question shortly after the presidential election of 1968.

Bertel M. Sparks, the uncle, worked his way out of "poverty stricken" Appalachia through law school and two graduate degrees in law. He served on the faculty of New York University School of Law for eighteen years and is now professor of law at Duke University. He is the author of two books and numerous articles in legal periodicals.

Dear Philip:

In reply to your question about my opinion of the Electoral College, I am in favor of retaining it. Before abolishing any institution that has been with us for such a long period, we should take time to ask why it came into existence in the first place, how it has worked in the past, and what substitute we have to offer. It is my opinion that a careful consideration of these questions will lead to the conclusion that the Electoral College is not so bad after all.

It seems that when our Founding Fathers were about the task of writing our Constitution they were almost unanimous on two basic ideas. They wanted a government strong enough to keep the peace and they feared any such government that was that strong. They had learned from their experience under King George that unlimited power in human hands was a dangerous thing. Being a highly educated group, their knowledge and understanding of history had taught them that tyrannical power was not confined to any one form of government. It could exist whether its form was that of a monarchy, aristocracy, theocracy, or even a democracy. Their experience under the Articles of Confederation had also taught them that a government without adequate power could not protect its citizens in the exercise of their commercial and social relations with each other. It was a recognition of these diverse and somewhat conflicting policy goals that led them to the establishment of a form of government that made possible the greatest exercise of personal freedom and the development of the highest level of material well-being that has ever been known anywhere else on the earth before or since. How did they do it?

The scheme agreed upon by that little group of men gathered in Philadelphia in 1787 was not a democracy but a republic, characterized by a separation of powers and a division of authority. To them this meant much more than a separation of the legislative, executive, and judicial departments of government. Regardless of what separation of the departments could be achieved, the men who were laying our foundation feared the consequences of having all three concentrated in one central government. That much had been tried before in various parts of the world, and under such arrangements tyranny had often been the ultimate result even where the election of the officials imposing the tyranny had been by popular choice. The added feature was a federal system where the local units of government, the states, were made independent entities and not just instrumentalities of the central power and the central government was made one of strictly limited powers.

The exercise of even such limited powers was carefully circumscribed. The Senate was to represent the states, with all states being equal for this purpose, and the House was to represent the people. The chief executive was not to be chosen by the legislative body, as is the custom in many countries of the world, but was made independent of them. Yet the power he could exercise without their approval was strictly confined. Although the judges were to be appointed by the President, they could not be removed by him and therefore it was highly unlikely that the judiciary would ever be dominated by any one President. It was no accident that the Representatives and Senators were given terms of different lengths and the election of Senators was so arranged that not more than one-third of them could be changing at any one time. And the President's term was made of different duration from that of either House or Senate. This somewhat awkward staggering of terms was to avoid the instability that could result from having the whole government change, even by popular vote, at a moment of great emotional upheaval.

The Electoral College was invented as a part, although maybe only a small part, of this general scheme of separation of powers and division of authority. It was a scheme for letting the people choose but at the same time avoiding some of the dangers inherent in a direct choice. Not the least of the dangers they had in mind was that in a time of national turbulence, such as we might be approaching at the present time, sufficient emotional excitement might be generated to elect a popular and glamorous personality such as a Julius Caesar or a Napoleon Bonaparte. Of course, these dangers exist under any system of government. The important question is under what system can the extent of the dangers be diminished?

Any present-day student of the American government knows that this system of separation and division of powers with each department and each political unit serving as a check on every other did not work out exactly as intended by the Founding Fathers. None of the three branches of the central government has ever behaved exactly as the founders anticipated, and the powers and responsibilities of the state governments have declined to a degree that would probably frighten any delegate to the Constitutional Convention out of his wits. The Senate was never an impartial body of wise men serving to check the popular passions likely to be present in the House. Both the chief executive and the courts quickly developed into something that would probably be unrecognizable by any but the most discerning of the Fathers. And it is doubtful if any of them anticipated the emergence of either political parties or the extensive administrative machinery that now plagues the central government. The Electoral College never became the uninstructed gathering of superior and sober men calmly deciding upon a suitable citizen to serve as the Chief Executive for the coming four years.

But the fact that the formal expectations of the Fathers were never realized should not blind us to the fact that the basic framework which they established has served us well for almost 200 years. The central core of the tradition they established is still with us and it is now our tradition. The Electoral College is part of that tradition. While it is not the representative body exercising an independent judgment as was originally intended, it does have a function to perform. It is at least an accounting device registering a summation of the will of the people on a state-by-state basis. Being on a state-by-state basis, and that not strictly according to population, it has some tendency to decrease the likelihood of a President winning primarily through an emotional appeal giving him an overwhelming advantage in one section but probably making him obnoxious to a majority of the voters in other parts of the country. It also makes it a little more difficult for one social or economic unit to become dominant. What is even more important in my mind, it continues to remind us that we are a federal republic whose separate political units still have vitality.

And after all these years is anyone in a position to say the Electoral College has produced any bad results? There have been a few instances when the electoral majority did not coincide with the popular majority and also two instances when the electors failed to elect anybody and the question was thrown into the House of Representatives. But can anyone rightly say that any of these instances have produced bad results? I believe not. And in each instance the matter was handled peacefully and without any substantial amount of public excitement. That within itself is no small accomplishment when it is remembered how frequently a change of administrations is accompanied by varying degrees of disorder in many foreign countries. It might even be pointed out that the two Presidents who were chosen by the House of Representatives, Thomas Jefferson and John Q. Adams, are regarded by many as being among our more able Presidents.

Much has been made of the unfortunate things that could happen under our present system. But in view of the fact that none of the feared disasters has ever happened, I wonder if the danger isn't more imaginary than real. I find it hard to argue against almost 200 years of uninterrupted success! Even if no candidate had received an electoral majority in 1968, is there any reason to believe a peaceful and satisfactory solution could not have been reached? Let's explore the possibilities.

First of all, the electors, except in a few states, are not legally bound to vote with the party that elected them. It is possible that if no candidate had won a majority on November 5, enough electors would have switched their allegiance to give somebody a majority when the electoral votes were cast. If that had been done, is there any reason to believe the result would not have been a reasonable one or that it would not have been accepted by the public? If the electors had stood by the candidates for which they had been chosen and nobody had received a majority, is there any reason to believe the House of Representatives would not have acted in a responsible fashion?

Even if the House had acted so irresponsibly as to fail to choose anyone, there is still another route to follow. In such a case the Vice-President is to serve as if he were President. The election of the Vice-President would be by the Senate. Would the Senate be so irresponsible as to fail to choose a Vice-President?

So it seems that in order for us to end up without a lawfully chosen President, the Electoral College, the House of Representatives, and the Senate would all have to act in an irrational and irresponsible way. And as we moved from one of these bodies to the other the failure of each would place that much more moral pressure upon the next and would dramatize to the public the serious-ness of the occasion. The period of uncertainty during which the matter was being resolved would tend to be a period of sober reflection. Tempers would cool a bit and the danger of rebellion would be lessened rather than increased. With so many safeguards in operation, it is unlikely that we would ever find ourselves without a lawfully chosen and reasonably acceptable Chief Executive. At least I haven't heard any other system proposed that holds greater promise of permanence and stability than has been demonstrated by the one we have.

Your Uncle,

Bert

1. If you were to write a letter to a relative explaining why you were for or against the Electoral College, what points would you bring up?

CONCLUSION

Our system of government was designed through debate, discussion, and careful shaping of institutions that complement and check one another's powers. Each part plays an important role in safeguarding democracy and ensuring the smooth transition of power, enacting legislation, and providing progress as we strive for a more fair and equal country. But the Founders also gave us the tools to alter their original design when needed, a fact that has created controversy along with the opportunity to make our union more perfect.

The Electoral College is one of those crucial parts of our government, designed as a check on presidential elections that architect Alexander Hamilton felt was necessary to keep authoritarian or otherwise unsuitable candidates from office. But it was also designed at a time when only a small percentage of Americans were allowed to vote, when communication of results took weeks and months, and when governance was still reserved for a small elite. As times have changed, the nature of the Electoral College has as well, and although in the past it was meant to serve as a check on presidential election results, today it can easily run counter to the popular vote and according to some even fail in its stated purpose—keeping the office of the presidency safe from those who might undermine democratic norms.

In recent years, there has been a public debate about the future and use of the Electoral College. Legislators, advocates, and voters who believe the time has come to do away with the system point out cases in which the Electoral College has resulted in the election of someone other than the winner of the popular vote as evidence that our voting system no longer requires a gatekeeping process; but those who favor keeping the Electoral College argue that centuries of tradition and the intent of the Founders needs to be taken into account before doing away with what has long been an integral part of our democracy.

Any changes to our voting system on the national level will take significant legislation and state-level ratification, so any possible changes to the Electoral College are years, if not decades, in the future. Right now, the debate centers mainly on whether or not those changes should be made at all, or if we should keep the system that was given to us by the Founding Fathers. What this debate shows, however, is just as important as any potential altering of our voting system; it shows that democracy, and our government, is a constant project that we can make better and more reflective of the times in which we live—which is what the Founders truly wanted for our country.

BIBLIOGRAPHY

Baca, et al. v. Hickenlooper, et al. United States Court of Appeals for the 10th Circuit, December 12, 2016. https://www.ca10 .uscourts.gov/opinions/14/14-1290.pdf.

Baker, Wayne. "Electoral College: Is it time to shake up the system?" *Read the Spirit:* Our Values. Retrieved June 5, 2018. https://www.readthespirit.com/ourvalues/electoral-college-is-it -time-to-shake-up-the-system.

Belenky, Alexander S. "Who Will Be the Next President? A Guide to the U.S. Presidential Election system." *DSpace@MIT*, 2013. https://dspace.mit.edu/handle/1721.1/108263.

Boxer, Barbara. "A Joint Resolution Proposing an Amendment to the Constitution of the United States to Abolish the Electoral College and to Provide for the Direction Popular Election of the President and Vice President of the United States." US Congress: Senate, November 15, 2016. https://www.congress .gov/bill/114th-congress/senate-joint-resolution/41.

Bush et al. v. Gore et al. US Supreme Court, December 12, 2000. https://supreme.justia.com/cases/federal/us/531/98.

Byrne, Bradley. "The Faithless Elector Problem." *Congressional Record,* January 9, 2017. https://www.congress.gov /congressional-record/2017/1/9/house-section/article /h197-4?q=%7B%22search%22%3A%5B%22electoral+col- lege%22%5D%7D&r=16.

Chavez, Aida. "Experts: Call for Electoral College Revolt Unlikely to Be Heeded in State." *Cronkite News*, December 16, 2016. https://cronkitenews.azpbs.org/2016/12/16/experts-call-for-elec- toral-college-revolt-unlikely-to-be-heeded-in-state.

Convers, Jr., John. "H.Con.Res.79 - Expressing the Sense of Congress that Congress and the States Should Consider a Constitutional Amendment to Reform the Electoral College and Establish a Process for Electing the President and Vice President by a National Popular Vote and Should Encour- age Individual States to Continue to Reform the Electoral College Process Through Such Steps as the Formation of an Interstate Compact to Award the Majority of Electoral College Votes to the National Popular Vote Winner." US Congress: House of Representatives, September 14, 2017. https://www.congress.gov/bill/115th-congress/house-concur- rent-resolution/79/text.

Cranston, Bryan. "How Is the American President Elected?" *Conversation,* October 25, 2016. https://theconversation .com/how-is-the-american-president-elected-67632.

Durran, Dale R. "Whose Votes Count the Least in the Electoral College?" *Conversation*, March 13, 2017 https://theconversation.com/whose-votes-count-the-least-in-the-electoral-college-74280.

Guelzo, Allen C. and James H. Hulme. "In Defense of the Electoral College." *Picking the President: Understanding the Electoral College*, edited by Eric Burin. Grand Forks, ND: The Digital Press at the University of North Dakota, 2017. http://cupola.gettysburg.edu/cgi/viewcontent.cgi?article=1095&context=cwfac.

MacGillis, Alec. "The Democrats' Bad Map." *ProPublica*, October 22, 2016. https://www.propublica.org/article/the-democrats-bad-map.

McPherson v. Blacker. US Supreme Court, October 17, 1892 http://cdn.loc.gov/service/ll/usrep/usrep146/usrep146001/usrep146001.pdf.

Merling, Lara and Dean Baker. "In the Electoral College White Votes Matter More." *Center for Economic and Policy Research*, November 13, 2016 http://cepr.net/blogs/beat-the-press/in-the-electoral-college-white-votes-matter-more.

Neale, Thomas H. "Electoral College Reform: Contemporary Issues for Congress." Congressional Research Service, October 6, 2017. https://fas.org/sgp/crs/misc/R43824.pdf.

Ray, Chairman of the State Democratic Executive Committee of Alabama v. Blair. US Supreme Court, April 15, 1952. http://cdn.loc.gov/service/ll/usrep/usrep343/usrep343214/usrep343214.pdf.

Reed, Lawrence W. "Keep the Electoral College." Foundation for Economic Education, March 1, 2001. https://fee.org/articles/keep-the-electoral-college/

Reid, Senator Harry. "The Electoral College." *Congressional Record,* November 16, 2016 https://www.congress.gov/congressional-record/2016/11/16/senate-section/article/s6387-7?q=%7B%22search%22%3A%5B%22electoral+college%22%5D%7D&r=93.

Sparks, Bertel. "Why Have an Electoral College?" Foundation for Economic Education, April 1, 1969. https://fee.org/articles/why-have-an-electoral-college.

Staff. "Our Plan." *EqualVotes*. Retrieved June 5, 2018. https://equalvotes.us.

Williams, Walter E. "Democracy or Republic?" Foundation for Economic Education, June 1, 2007. https://fee.org/articles/democracy-or-republic.

CHAPTER NOTES

CHAPTER 1: WHAT THE EXPERTS SAY

"ELECTORAL COLLEGE REFORM: CONTEMPORARY ISSUES FOR CONGRESS" BY THOMAS H. NEALE

[Editor's note: Due to the length of these chapter notes, they can be found with the original article.]

EXCERPT FROM "WHO WILL BE THE NEXT PRESIDENT? A GUIDE TO THE U.S. PRESIDENTIAL ELECTION SYSTEM" BY ALEXANDER S. BELENKY

1. Belenky, A., Understanding the Fundamentals of the U.S. Presidential Election System. Springier, Heidelberg, New York, Dordrecht, London, 2012.
2. Broder, D., Electoral "Fixes," the Washington Post, October 21, 2004; Page A29.
3. Why the Electoral College Is So Hard to Understand, June 29, 2014 http://bibowen.hubpages.com/hub/founders-electoral-college
4. Fortier, J. (ed) After the People Vote: a Guide to the Electoral College, AEI Press, Washington D.C., 2004.
5. Koza, J., Fadem, B., Grueskin, M., Mandell, M., Richie, R., Zimmerman, J., Every Vote Equal: A State-Based Plan For Electing The President By National Popular Vote, National Popular Vote Press, 2011.
6. Peirce, N., The People's President. The Electoral College in American History and the Direct-Vote Alternative, Simon & Shuster, New York, 1968.
7. Peirce, N., Longley, L., The People's President. The Electoral College in American History and the Direct-Vote Alternative. Revised Edition., Yale University Press, 1981.
8. Edwards III, G. Why the Electoral College Is Bad for America. Yale University Press, 2004. [...]

18. Belenky, A., How America Chooses Its Presidents. Second Edition, AuthorHouse, Bloomington & Milton Keynes, 2009.

22. Belenky, A., Extreme Outcomes of US Presidential Elections: The Logic of Appearance, Examples, Approaches to Eliminating NISTRAMAN Consulting, Brookline, MA, 2003.

[...]

31. Leip, D. Dave Leip's Atlas of U.S. Presidential Elections, http://us-electionatlas.org/

32. Belenky, A. The good, the bad, and the ugly: three proposals to introduce the nationwide popular vote in U.S. presidential elections, Michigan Law Review, 106, p.110-116, February, 2008.

33. Belenky, A. Alexander S. Belenky: Brittle corner stones of national popular vote plan \Providence Journal, April 11, 2009.

[...]

78. Cronke R. Hicks, J., Re-examining Voter Confidence as a Metric for Election Performance. Reed College and Early Voting Information Center, 2010.

79. Voter Fraud, Intimidation and Suppression in the 2004 President Election, American Center for Voting Rights, Legislative Fund, July 21, 2005.

80. Ceci, S., Kain, E., Jumping on the bandwagon with the underdog: the impact of attitude polls on polling nbehavior, Public Opinion Quarterly, Volume 46, Issue 2, 1982.

81. Linton, M., Making Votes Count: Case for ElectoralReforms, Profile Books., London, UK, 1998. https://www.amazon.com/Making-Votes-Count-ElectoralReform/dp/1861970870/ref=sr_1_fkmr0_1?ie=UTF8&qid=1472994876&sr=8-1-fkmr0&keywords=Making+Votes+Count.+Profile+-Books.%2C+London%2C+UK%2C+1998

82. Madhani, A., Voter-ID laws may handicap black voter turnout, Dems fear. USA Today, July 11, 2012.

83. Underhill, W., Voter Identification Requirements | Voter ID Laws, http://www.ncsl.org/research/elections-and-campaigns/voter-id.aspx#Details

84. Belenky, A., Larson, R., To Queue or Not to Queue? In a U.S. presidential election, that should NOT be a question \ OR/MS Today 33 (3), p. 30-35, 2006.

85. Belenky A., Larson, R., Faulty system for democracy, The Boston Herald, February 10, 2007.

86. Belenky, A., Larson, R., Voting shouldn't require a heroic act of patience, The Christian Science Monitor, September 12, 2006.

87. Help America Vote Act of 2002, Public Law 107-252, 107th Congress, October 29, 2002.

88. Belenky, A., Larson, R., Voting standards are the key to avoiding long lines on Election Day, Plain Dealer, May 8, 2009.

89. Fair, R. Predicting Presidential Elections and Other Things, Second Edition, Stanford Economics and Finance, 2011.

90. Stewart III, C., Voting Technologies, American Review of Political Science, Volume 14, p.353-378, 2011.

91. Kumar, S., Walia, E., Analysis of Electronic Voting Systems in Several Countries, International Journal on Computer Science and Engineering, Volume 3, 5, 2011.

92. Bachner, J., From Classroom to Voting Booth: The Effect of High School Civic Education on Turnout, September 12, 2010. http://www.gov.harvard.edu/files/Bachner%20Civic%20Education%20Article.pdf

93. Kiousis S., McDevitt, M., Agenda Setting in Civic Development. Effect of Curricula and Issue Importance on Youth Voter Turnout, Communication Research, p. 1-22, 2008.

94. Chandler, D., Galts, C. MIT launches student-produced educational video initiative, MIT News, April 25, 2012. http://web.mit.edu/newsoffice/2012/k-12-education-video-initiative-0425.html

95. ProCon http://2012election.procon.org/view.resource.php?resourceID=004483

96. GALLUP http://www.gallup.com/poll/188096/democratic-republican-identification-nearhistorical-lows.aspx

97. League of Women Voters, http://lwv.org/press-releases/league-refuses-help-perpetratefraud

98. Federal Election Commission, FEC Record: Litigation, http://www.fec.gov/

99. Easley, J. and Kamisar B., Third-party candidates face uphill climb to get place on presidential debate stage, The Hill, May 12, 2016.

100. Commission on Presidential Debates. Commission on Presidential Debates Announces 2016 Nonpartisan Candidate Selection Criteria, Forms Working Group on Format, Oct, 29, 2015 http://www.debates.org/index.php?mact=News,cntnt01,-detail,0&cntnt01articleid=58&cntnt01origid=15&cntnt01detail-template=newspage&cntnt01returnid=80

101. Wright, D. Poll: Trump, Clinton score historic unfavorable ratings, CNN Politics, March 22, 2016 http://edition.cnn.com/2016/03/22/politics/2016-election-poll-donald-trumphillary-clinton/

102. Change the Rule, http://www.changetherule.org/

103. G. Farah, No Debate: How the Republican and Democratic Parties Secretly Control the Presidential Debates, Seven Stories Press, 2004

104. B. Montopoli, Do the debates unfairly shut out third parties?, CBS News, October 1

CHAPTER 3: WHAT THE COURTS SAY

EXCERPT FROM *BUSH ET AL. V. GORE ET AL.*, FROM THE US SUPREME COURT

1 Similarly, our jurisprudence requires us to analyze the "background principles" of state property law to determine whether there has been a taking of property in violation of the Takings Clause. That constitutional guarantee would, of course, afford no protection against state power if our inquiry could be concluded by a state supreme court holding that state property law accorded the plaintiff no rights. See *Lucas v. South Carolina Coastal Council*, 505 U. S. 1003 (1992). In one of our oldest cases, we similarly made an independent evaluation of state law in order to protect federal treaty guarantees. In *Fairfax's Devisee v. Hunter's Lessee*, 7 Cranch 603 (1813), we disagreed with the Supreme Court of Appeals of Virginia that a 1782 state law had extinguished the property interests of one Denny Fairfax, so that a 1789 ejectment order against Fairfax supported by a 1785 state law did not constitute a future confiscation under the 1783 peace treaty with Great Britain. See *id.*, at 623; *Hunter v. Fairfax's Devisee*, 1 Mum. 218 (Va. 1809).

2 We vacated that decision and remanded that case; the Florida Supreme Court reissued the same judgment with a new opinion on December 11, 2000, *Palm Beach County Canvassing Bd. v. Harris*, 772 So. 2d 1273.

3 Specifically, the Florida Supreme Court ordered the Circuit Court to include in the certified vote totals those votes identified for Vice President Gore in Palm Beach County and Miami-Dade County.

4 It is inconceivable that what constitutes a vote that must be counted under the "error in the vote tabulation" language of the protest phase is different from what constitutes a vote that must be counted under the "legal votes" language of the contest phase.

BACA, ET AL. V. HICKENLOOPER, ET AL., FROM UNITED STATES COURT OF APPEALS FOR THE 10TH CIRCUIT

[1] This latter provision has been interpreted to grant Congress power over Presidential elections coextensive with that which Article I section 4 grants it over congressional elections. *Burroughs v. United States*, 290 U.S. 534 (1934).

[2] Instead, plaintiffs point primarily to statements made by Alexander Hamilton in The Federalist No. 68. E.g., Dist. Ct. Docket No. 2 at 6; Emergency Motion at 10. Although we turn to external sources when unable to discern the meaning of the Constitution from its plain language, we begin our analysis with careful examination of the words used. Here, plaintiffs make no textual argument, at all. This is not to say that there is no language in Article II or the Twelfth 3 Amendment that might ultimately support plaintiffs' position. See *Ray v. Blair*, 343 U.S. 214, 232 (1952) ("No one faithful to our history can deny that the plan originally contemplated, *what is implicit in its text*, that electors would be free agents, to exercise an independent and nonpartisan judgment as to the men best qualified for the Nation's highest offices." (emphasis added)). For example, there is language in the Twelfth Amendment that could arguably support the plaintiffs' position. *E.g.*, Michael Stokes Paulsen, *The Constitutional Power of the Electoral College*, Public Discourse (Nov. 21, 2016) (available at www.thepublicdiscourse.com/2016/11/18283/). But it is not our role to make those arguments for them.

4. And we deem such an attempt by the State unlikely in light of the text of the Twelfth Amendment.

CHAPTER 4: WHAT THE ADVOCATES SAY

"IN DEFENSE OF THE ELECTORAL COLLEGE" BY ALLEN GUELZO AND JAMES H. HULME

* A version of this essay appeared as Allen Guelzo and James Hulme, "In defense of the Electoral College," *PostEverything* (blog), *Washington Post*, November 15, 2016, http://www .washingtonpost.com/posteverything/wp/2016/11/15/in -defense-of-the-electoral-college

GLOSSARY

battleground states—States with close margins of victory between parties where candidates often spend significant resources and time during their campaigns.

congressional district method—A system of allocating electors that relies on voting totals in districts rather than assigning all votes to one candidate based on the voting total for the state as a whole.

direct popular election—The election of the president and vice president through national voting rather than the Electoral College.

disenfranchise—To take away either directly or through covert means the right of a person to vote.

Electoral College—The process by which state delegates vote for and elect the president and vice president.

Electoral College "lock"—The belief that one party or another has a stronghold on the Electoral College over the course of multiple elections.

electors—State-appointed delegates to the Electoral College.

faithless electors—Electors who vote against the expectation of the state they represent.

indirect—A voting system in which the citizens do not elect a leader through popular vote.

mandamus—A command from a higher court issued to a lower court.

National Popular Vote—A movement joined by multiple states to pledge their electors to the winner of the popular vote rather than the state vote.

popular vote—The result of the national election, which does not necessarily match the Electoral College result.

swing states—States with very close margins of victory between parties, meaning that they could vote either way during an election cycle.

Twelfth Amendment—The amendment to the Constitution introduced in 1789 that outlined the way the Electoral College would function.

voter turnout—The percentage of eligible voters who take part in an election.

winner-takes-all—A system of allocating electors' votes by which the candidate with the most votes in a state receives all of that state's votes.

FURTHER READING

BOOKS

Burin, Eric. *Picking the President: Understanding the Electoral College*. Grand Forks, ND: Digital Press at the University of North Dakota, 2017.

Edwards III, George C. *Why the Electoral College is Bad for America*. New Haven, CT: Yale University Press, 2011.

Gregg, Gary L. *Securing Democracy: Why We Have An Electoral College*. Wilmington, VT: Intercollegiate Studies Institute, 2008.

Michener, James A. *Presidential Lottery: The Reckless Gamble of Our Electoral System*. New York, NY: Dial Press, 2014.

Peterson, Josiah. *The Electoral College: Critical to our Republic*. New York, NY: The King's College Press, 2017.

Ross, Tara. *The Indispensable Electoral College: How the Founders' Plan Saves Our Country from Mob Rule*. New York, NY: Gateway Books, 2017.

WEBSITES

The National Archives and Records Administration
https://www.archives.gov
This federal resource houses and digitizes documents of national importance, including the Declaration of Independence. Digital copies of important historical documents can be found on its website.

The National Center for Constitutional Studies [NCCS]
https://nccs.net
NCCS seeks to raise awareness and education about the Constitution through courses and resources that are included on its website.

INDEX

ABOUT THE EDITOR

Bridey Heing is a writer and book critic based in Washington, DC. She holds degrees in political science and international affairs from DePaul University and Washington University in Saint Louis. Her areas of focus are comparative politics and Iranian politics. Her masters' thesis explores the evolution of populist politics and democracy in Iran since 1900. She has written about Iranian affairs, women's rights, and art and politics for publications like the *Economist*, *Hyperallergic*, and the *Establishment*. She also writes about literature and film. She enjoys traveling, reading, and exploring Washington, DC's many museums.